THE MANAGEMENT OF INTERNATIONAL ENTERPRISES

The Management of International Enterprises

A Socio-Political View

Monir H. Tayeb
Heriot-Watt University
Edinburgh

First published in Great Britain 2000 by
MACMILLAN PRESS LTD
Houndmills, Basingstoke, Hampshire RG21 6XS and London
Companies and representatives throughout the world

A catalogue record for this book is available from the British Library.

ISBN 0–333–74886–7

 First published in the United States of America 2000 by
ST. MARTIN'S PRESS, INC.,
Scholarly and Reference Division,
175 Fifth Avenue, New York, N.Y. 10010

ISBN 0–312–23121–0

Library of Congress Cataloging-in-Publication Data
Tayeb, Monir H.
The management of international enterprises : a socio-political view / Monir Tayeb.
p.   cm.
Includes bibliographical references and index.
ISBN 0–312–23121–1 (cloth)
1. International business enterprises—Management.   2. Multiculturalism.
I. Title.

HD62.4 .T39   2000
658'.049—dc21
                                                                99–054952

This book is printed on paper suitable for recycling and made from fully managed and sustained forest sources.

10   9   8   7   6   5   4   3   2   1
09   08   07   06   05   04   03   02   01   00

Printed and bound in Great Britain by
Antony Rowe Ltd, Chippenham, Wiltshire

Contents

List of Tables

Introduction

This book addresses major issues related to international enterprises and the world in which they operate from a socio-political perspective. There are many worthy publications in this field, mainly focused on the economic and managerial angles, and they have all been an inspiration behind the current book. The author has attempted to build a coherent picture of the 'life' of an international, indeed multinational, firm, from the factors which contribute to its birth and later to its 'personal' characteristics, to the myriad challenges that it faces once up and running. The book draws on the author's relevant theoretical and empirical research experience accumulated over two decades or so, and spanning a number of countries in Asia, Europe and north America. In addition, the research findings and theoretical arguments of other scholars are of course drawn and built upon. The intention throughout the book is to discuss and analyse the issues involved rather than to prescribe what multinational firms should or should not do; I shall not be so presumptuous. That is the prerogative of the managers and workforces of those firms, who, judging by the available evidence, are doing a fine job.

The book consists of two parts. Part I includes Chapters 1 to 4 and sets the scene for internationalisation. Chapter 1 discusses major historical and current economic, political and cultural factors that could lead to the competitive advantage of some nations over others in the international market. A discussion on the membership of global and regional political-economic organisations, a policy pursued by many countries, is also included here. The aim is to illustrate the way in which such policies could contribute to a nation's standing in the international market, and to examine whether or not those nations that are not part of regional or global organisations are at a disadvantage as a result. The chapter will include examples of both successful and unsuccessful nations to illustrate the relationship between the above factors and their current standing in the business world. The success of these nations will be judged according to both economic and non-economic indicators, such as the state of health, literacy rate, per capita income and energy, pattern of income distribution, presence of their companies and products in the international market, and the like.

Chapter 2 explores the notion of the home county as a launch pad for internationalisation. Nations are both homes and hosts to international firms. The first section of the chapter discusses the national factors, such as foreign trade polices, which 'prompt' or encourage companies to contemplate the expansion of their operations beyond their domestic market into overseas regions. Nations, as hosts, could adopt certain policies, based on their political-economic priorities, which aim to attract foreign firms. The rationale behind these policies and their likely effects on the host nations, such as employment, technological advancement and cultural changes, are dealt with in the second section of the chapter. Policies pursued by nations both as home and host could determine the specific form that internationalisation of an enterprise might take. These are discussed and illustrated with appropriate examples.

Chapter 3 looks at the issue of internal organisational competencies as launch pads for internationalisation. Here organisational factors such as managerial competence, technological know-how, and financial and human resources that enable certain companies to internationalise their operations are discussed. Chapters 1 and 2 discuss, among other things, the resources that are available to potential users, such as a well-educated workforce, tax breaks and political stability. Chapter 3 examines the international companies' ability to exploit and utilise these resources to their advantage.

The last chapter in Part I explores why certain firms decide to expand overseas in the first place and reviews different motivations that they might have for becoming multinational. Furthermore, the chapter examines whether or not there are limits to internationalisation and indeed globalisation.

The second part of the book, containing Chapters 5 to 9, explores the implications of socio-political 'forces' for the management of an international firm. The discussion covers topics such as relationships with the external environment, strategic development, organisational design, human resource management and company culture in respective chapters. Part II begins by reminding the reader of the various forms that internationalisation might take, ranging from simple export and import business to setting up and running wholly-owned production subsidiaries abroad. Also, the extent of internationalisation could vary from involvement in one or two neighbouring countries, to multinational operations, to global enterprises. This brief introduction is necessary because the issues discussed in Chapters 5 to 9 will have different implications for international firms depending on the form and the extent of their international involvement. In addition, the type of products or services that these firms produce and sell and the customers they serve will have significant implications for the ways in which they deal with their environment and the ways in which they run their internal affairs. A firm that makes and sells arms to several countries around the world faces a different challenge from the one that sells teddy bears to a few neighbouring nations.

Chapter 5 identifies various parts of what is in effect a patchwork context within which international firms operate: governments, suppliers, customers and partners, all with different values, preferences, policies and priorities. International firms have to respond to the challenges posed by this context; they also help shape it in some ways. Chapters 6 to 9 all begin by defining the concepts and phenomena with which they are concerned. They then proceed by discussing what characteristics and features these might take as far as international companies are concerned, given their wider social, cultural, political and economic contexts. Some chapters in this part also explore how international companies try to maintain their integrity as a single entity while allowing for responsiveness to their differentiated environments, by adjusting and readjusting their strategies, operations and other organisational characteristics.

Finally, Chapter 10 brings together the various discussions and arguments presented in the book.

MONIR H. TAYEB

Part I
Internationalisation:
Setting the Scene

1 The Significance of Socio-Political Influences on International Business Development

INTRODUCTION

This chapter discusses major historical and current economic, political and cultural factors that could lead to the competitive advantage of some nations over others in the international market. The chapter includes examples of both successful and unsuccessful nations to illustrate the relationship between these factors and their current standing in the business world. The success of these nations will be judged according to both economic and non-economic indicators, such as the state of health, literacy rate, per capita income and energy, pattern of income distribution, presence of their companies and products in the international market, and the like.

Currently, although the world is no longer divided along political and ideological lines, it is still divided into 'haves' and 'have nots'. In historical terms we are still close to a time when the world was dominated by no more than a dozen powers from what we now term the North (Arnold, 1989). Much of the rest of the world belongs to the South. The 'haves' are the rich industrialised countries mainly situated in the northern hemisphere. They are characterised by high per capita income, high GNP, the manufacture of semi-processed and finished goods, the use of computers, capital-intensive technology, high per capita consumption of electricity and other sources of energy, a low level of natural resources relative to less-industrialised nations, mechanised agriculture, high rates of literacy, and long life expectancy.

The 'have nots' are the poor countries with predominantly agricultural economies mainly situated in the southern hemisphere. They are characterised by dense population, low per capita income, a low rate of literacy, high rates of infant mortality, short life expectancy, largely non-mechanised agriculture, and the export of usually one and sometimes two commodities, such as crude oil and cash crops. Given the disadvantages suffered by people in the 'have not' group and their

3

exposure, through mass media, to the riches enjoyed by the inhabitants of the 'have' nations, it is natural that they would wish to catch up with them or at least to go someway towards achieving a decent standard of living.

In the modern world, as it has always been throughout history, to have a fulfilling domestic life nations have had to be successful on the international scene, either through wars and conquests or trade or both. National competitive advantage, in other words, has been the rule of the game from the beginning, however nationhood is defined at any point in time. In our own century the end of the Cold War in late 1989 ushered in a new era in which new criteria for national competitiveness were set down. As Lehmann (1998) points out, the end of the Cold War can be seen as leading to a crucial transformation from geopolitics to geoeconomics. The global rivalry between nations, in other words, is no longer about conventional sources of power (military might, territory, political clout, ideology), but about fundamentally, indeed exclusively, economic sources of power. These include technology, management skills, industrial bases, capital, government–industry relations and so on. This and later chapters will examine how various nations fare on these and similar criteria.

NATIONAL COMPETITIVENESS

We know that nations which succeed in the international market are those which not only have a competitive advantage on certain factors of production, but are also able to manage these factors in such a way as to translate their potential advantage to an actual one. This point was especially noted in Porter's seminal study (1990). In his national 'diamond', Porter considered four sets of conditions/characteristics as playing determinant roles in a nation's international success:

1. *Factor conditions.* The nation's position in factors of production, such as skilled labour or infrastructure, necessary to compete in a given industry.
2. *Demand conditions.* The nature of home demand for the industry's product or service.
3. *Related and supporting industries.* The presence or absence in the nation of supplier industries and related industries that are internationally competitive.

4. *Firm strategy, structure and rivalry*. The conditions in the nation governing how companies are created, organised and managed, and the nature of domestic rivalry.

Porter placed his emphasis on industry advantages, rather than on the national advantage as a whole. It is argued here, in line with Francis's argument (1992), that there are national differences in competitiveness and not just differences in where competitive advantage lies. None of the countries that Porter included in his sample was a non-runner. That is to say, had he also included countries like Pakistan and Bangladesh he would have observed that these latter nations are not competitive internationally at any level, be it firm, industry or nation (Tayeb, 1995). All 'Porter's countries' are major players in the international market.

Moreover, Porter argues for the significant role that governments' policies play in helping along with the competitive advantage of their nations, but he underemphasises, if any, the role of another great institution, the national culture, in both the creation and maintenance of national competitiveness. Take, for example, a highly competitive nation like Japan and a non-competitive one like Iran. It is true that some Japanese industries, such as electronics and car manufacturing, are more competitive than some of its other industries. But it is also true that the country as a whole is very competitive and successful also. Iran, by contrast, does not have any internationally competitive industry – Iran's export of crude oil which is a finite natural resource does not of course fall into this category.

There must, therefore, be something about such non-competitive countries which sets them back, and something about such countries as Japan that sets them forth. The human resource, for instance, is a national asset whose quality constitutes a crucial ingredient here and whose management makes a difference between nations. A hard-working, motivated, committed and skilled workforce whose energies and qualities are nourished and channelled appropriately could elevate a nation's economic performance to higher plains. As will be discussed later, there are certain culturally-rooted attitudes and values which are helpful in building up a nation's standing in the world, and certain others which could severely hinder such standing, at both macro and micro levels.

In this connection, Tayeb (1995) argued that a reinterpretation of the findings of published comparative cross-cultural studies of management reveals that countries like Japan, the United States, the so-called Asian Tigers, and those in Western Europe enjoy high-repertoire national cultures. In each of these nations all forms and sizes of organisation flourish, with a wide range of human resource and other management strategies and practices to match their employees' predispositions, products and markets. Each nation as a whole is a major player in the international market, a position firmly supported by a rich foundation. In contrast, countries like Iraq, India, Cuba and many of their fellow third-world nations provide their business firms with a context which constrains their movements and restricts their options both in their strategic and operative activities. These nations are orchestras with limited domestic repertoires and a minute or non-existent international repertoire.

In a similar vein, Lane (1995), in a comparison of French, British and German domestic and international companies, found that they were heavily embedded in the social, economic and political institutions of their respective home nations. There was a constant interaction between firms and markets on the one hand, and social institutions on the other, which Lane conceptualised as national industrial order. Furthermore, she argues, the strong concern for the social embeddedness of economic structures and processes has necessarily led to an emphasis on the national distinctiveness of industrial orders and their historical shaping and reproduction. Moreover, as Lehmann (1998) points out, in earlier decades it was often claimed that it is companies, not countries, that compete against each other. This was never entirely true: countries did compete against each other, some more aggressively and some more successfully than others.

Japan, South Korea, France, Germany, Sweden, the USA and others established government–corporate alliances under various guises via industrial policies, subsidies and so on. These alliances were aimed at combining strengths to gain competitive advantage in international markets. Such efforts were by no means invariably crowned with success. The point is that, Lehmann argues, when nations sought to compete, they did so essentially by erecting platforms to launch domestic companies ('national champions') to predominance through technology, exports, the industrial base or a combination of some or all of these. It is important to note that it is not argued here that all the firms operating in competitive nations will inevitably be successful players in the international market. Rather, as will be discussed in a later chapter, competitive nations are able to provide a high repertoire for their domestic firms to choose from, but it is up to these firms' internal strength and competence to avail themselves of this high repertoire and all the potentials it offers. John Child's (1972) notion of strategic choice is also

Table 1.1   Indicators of national performance, 1996

Countries	GDP (ppp) growth %	Per capita GDP $US	Literacy rate %		Life expectancy		Infant mortality per 1000 live births	Per capita electricity consumption kwh
			Men	Women	Men	Women		
Europe and US								
Germany	1.4	20 400	99	99	74	80	5	5 727
France	1.3	20 900	99	99	75	83	6	6 278
United Kingdom	2.4	20 400	99	99	75	80	6	5 198
United States	2.4	28 600	97	97	73	79	7	11 636
Southeast Asia								
Japan	3.6	22 700	99	99	77	84	4	6 895
Hong Kong	4.7	26 000	96	88	76	82	5	3 716
Singapore	6.5	21 200	96	86	75	80	4	7 002
South Korea	6.9	14 200	99	97	70	76	8	3 563
Taiwan	5.7	14 700	93	79	74	81	7	5 270
Well on their way								
Czech Republic	5.0	11 100	99	99	70	77	7	4 712
Hungary	0.5	7 500	99	98	66	75	10	3 200
Poland	6.0	6 400	99	98	68	77	14	3 124
Malaysia	8.2	10 750	89	78	67	73	23	1 983
Mexico	5.1	8 100	92	87	70	78	24	1 206
Thailand	6.7	7 700	96	92	65	73	32	1 205
Brazil	2.9	6 300	83	83	57	66	53	1 572
Hopeful but a long way to go								
Russia	-6.0	5 200	100	97	58	72	24	5 114
Iran	3.6	5 200	78	66	66	69	51	1 137
Indonesia	7.0	3 770	90	78	60	64	61	276
China	9.7	2 800	90	73	69	72	38	684
Philippines	5.5	2 600	95	94	63	69	35	326
India	6.5	1 600	66	38	62	63	66	412

* Purchasing power parity.
Sources: United nations, World Bank and CIA documents and Internet sites.

relevant here. The flip side of this argument is that in non-competitive nations one sometimes hears of firms which have built up world-class competence and strength often in spite of their home nation – India's Tata and Reliance are examples of this kind.

The present chapter builds on Porter's model by concentrating on competitiveness at the national level. The objective is to explore the role of nations as launching pads for their companies, and the ways in which this role is fulfilled or falters because of political, cultural and similar features which make up a nation's identity and character. As a starting point, Table 1.1 compares a sample of nations on their economic and non-economic performance records, and Table 1.2 shows major exports of the same nations. The tables include various groups of nations from around the world, in different categories. Although the nations included in each category are listed according to their per capita GDP, their real performance records should be judged in the light of all the indicators as a whole.

Table 1.2   Major exports of a selected group of nations

Country	Commodities
Germany	Manufactures 88.2 % (including machines and machine tools, chemicals, motor vehicles, iron and steel products), agricultural products 5.0 %, raw materials 2.3 %, fuels 1.0 %, other 3.5 %
France	Machinery and transportation equipment, chemicals, foodstuffs, agricultural products, iron and steel products, textiles and clothing
United Kingdom	Manufactured goods, machinery, fuels, chemicals, semi-finished goods, transport equipment
United States	Capital goods, automobiles, industrial supplies and raw materials, consumer goods, agricultural products
Japan	Manufactures 96 % (including machinery 50 %, motor vehicles 19 %, consumer electronics 3 %)
Hong Kong	Clothing, textiles, yarn and fabric, footwear, electrical appliances, watches and clocks, toys
Singapore	Computer equipment, rubber and rubber products, petroleum products, telecommunications equipment
South Korea	Electronic and electrical equipment, machinery, steel, automobiles, ships, textiles, clothing, footwear, fish

Taiwan	Electronic and electrical equipment, machinery, steel, automobiles, ships, textiles, clothing, footwear, fish
Czech Republic	Manufactured goods 32.4 %, machinery and transport equipment 26.3 %, chemicals 10.4 %, raw materials and fuel 11.3 %
Hungary	Raw materials 39.5 %, consumer goods 25.0 %, agriculture and food products 21.8 %, machinery and equipment 11.3 %, fuels and electricity 2.4 %
Poland	Intermediate goods 38 %, machinery and transport equipment 23 %, consumer goods 21 %, foodstuffs 10 %, fuels 7 %
Malaysia	Electronic equipment, petroleum and petroleum products, palm oil, wood and wood products, rubber, textiles
Mexico	Crude oil, oil products, coffee, silver, engines, motor vehicles, cotton, consumer electronics
Thailand	Manufactures 73 %, agricultural products and fisheries 21 %, raw materials 5 %, fuels 1 %
Brazil	Iron ore, soybean bran, orange juice, footwear, coffee, motor vehicle parts
Russia	Petroleum and petroleum products, natural gas, wood and wood products, metals, chemicals, and a wide variety of civilian and military manufactures
Iran	Petroleum 85 %, carpets, fruits, nuts, hides, iron, steel
Indonesia	Manufactures 51.9 %, fuels 26.4 %, foodstuffs 12.7 %, raw materials 9.0 %
China	Clothing, miscellaneous consumer goods, fabrics, footwear, toys, electrical machinery and switchgear
Philippines	Electronics, textiles, coconut products, telecommunications equipment, fruit, fish
India	Clothing, gems and jewellery, engineering goods, chemicals, leather manufactures, cotton yarn, and fabric

Sources: United nations, World Bank and CIA documents and Internet sites.

Of the nations listed in the tables, the United States, Japan, Germany and France, are, respectively, the first through fourth largest economies; they are clearly successful on both commercial and non-commercial criteria. This is not of course to deny that they do not have social or economic problems. The US has, for instance, her Harlem, and France her homeless and socially excluded, and Japan her unemployed street dwellers. But the general pattern is that of prosperity and of a high standard of living. Hong Kong, South Korea, Singapore and Taiwan have also made it to the rank of successful nations, notwithstanding the current economic crisis which cannot, of course, be a permanent feature of their economies. (OECD and IMF have now officially declared these countries as developed nations.) Their highly efficient and skilled workforces, well-established industrial and service sectors, and advanced physical and information infrastructure will pull them through this and future difficulties.

In fact the recovery has already started for some of these nations. According to a report published in *The Economist* (29 August 1998, p. 74) in South Korea, Thailand and even Indonesia, all of which suffered big currency devaluations, the volume of exports has risen by 20–30 per cent over the previous year. The rising export volumes will help to prop up output and jobs. J. P. Morgan, an American bank, reckons that this could lay a foundation for recovery in 1999 and 2000; it forecasts modest growth of around 2.5 per cent in both Thailand and South Korea in 1999, after a fall in output of around 6 per cent in 1998.

Already the export recovery, combined with a sharp cut in imports as domestic demand has slumped, has brought a huge improvement in some economies' current-account balances. South Korea ran a current-account surplus of $22 billion in the first half of 1998 (equivalent to almost 16% of GDP), compared with a deficit of $10 billion in the same period of 1997. Thailand ran a surplus of about $6 billion (12% of GDP) in the first five months of 1999, against a deficit of more than $4 billion in the comparable months of 1997.

The dramatic turnaround in trade balances, combined with loans from the International Monetary Fund and a cautious resumption of private capital inflows, has allowed some governments to start rebuilding foreign reserves. South Korea's, for example, have risen from a low of $5 billion in mid-December 1997 to a record high of $41 billion in June 1998. By April 1999 the IMF announced that the South Asian nations had overcome their crisis and recovered from the severe recession that they suffered in 1998 (*Le Monde*, 21 April 1999).

In the 'well on their way' category of Table 1.1 are included three ex-socialist countries of eastern Europe, which are to be shortly admitted to the EU club; the other four are still struggling but are heading in the right direction. Mexico, having suffered greatly in the early 1980s, embarked on a successful restructuring and reform of its economy, with the help of loans from the IMF and the rescheduling of its foreign debts.

Brazil already has an advanced manufacturing base. Malaysia and Thailand are not such star performers as the first wave of the so-called tigers, but they benefit from an educated workforce and openly welcome foreign investment. The ex-socialist countries have a high record on those fronts too, and have especially been able to attract foreign direct investment on a massive scale, which is of great help with the rebuilding of their economies.

The last group of nations in Table 1.1 is a 'mixed bag'. China, possibly an economic superpower of the twenty-first century, has made great strides since the 1980s by gradually opening its boundaries to foreign investment and trade. However, it still has a long way to go to get into the top rank: her hinterland is still largely untouched by the 'economic miracle' which is sweeping through some of its coastal regions; the workforce, although educated, still needs a great deal of training; a vast majority of enterprises are still state-owned and managed inefficiently; corruption, especially in the public sector, the army and among party officials, is rampant. Russia, a former military superpower, suffers from serious political and economic problems. The fall of the 'iron curtain' exposed its ramshackle economy which was hitherto hidden from the non-connoisseurs on the capitalist side of the curtain. Of the other four nations in this group, Indonesia and the Philippines have at least the advantage of open-door trade policies and welcoming attitudes towards foreign investors, in addition to a reasonably highly educated workforce. By contrast, Iran and India are still running their economies on a protectionist model notwithstanding the latter's recent 'reluctant' attempts to open up its door slightly and to reform its economy.

In the remainder of the present chapter some of the major historical, political and cultural reasons for the discrepancies among these nations will be explored and discussed. Given the scope of the task and limitations of space, the focus will be placed on a small group of nations, both successful and unsuccessful ones, but references to others will also be made where appropriate to illustrate various points and arguments.

HISTORICAL EVENTS AND NATIONAL COMPETITIVENESS

Industrial revolution, which started in mid-eighteenth century England, is an appropriate point to examine the roots of the modern economic and political configuration of the world. It heralded a new dawn which, although it was a culmination of perhaps the previous three centuries, has drastically changed the way people have lived and worked ever since.

The Industrial Revolution fed on the intellectual and scientific advances of the Age of Enlightenment and, in turn, stimulated a wave of scientific ideas and engineering inventions which changed agriculture as well as methods of production of goods. Mechanisation replaced and/or complemented manual labour in the farms and on the shop-floors. The ownership of the means of production began to be separated from its control, and feudal societies, based on a paternalistic master–serf structure, changed to class-based societies in which the middle class was the dominant elite. They either owned the means of production or acted on behalf of the owning classes. The working classes possessed only their labour which they exchanged for wages.

This division of roles, that is the ownership and control of the means of production on the one hand, and the provision of primary commodity – in this case labour – in exchange for money on the other, was to a large extent mirrored on the international scene which was to come. Britain and other early-comers to the industrialised world, such as western European countries and later the United States dominated the world of business in the following two centuries. By the end of the nineteenth century, Britain, with its empire greatly expanded, was the political and economic superpower of the world, the USA and recently reconstituted Germany were catching up fast, and the rest of the world were struggling, some looking more hopeful than others. By the close of the twentieth century, a few changes have taken place on the top, but the vast majority of nations are still struggling.

In an interesting comparison between these two points in time, *The Economist* (20 December, 1997, pp. 77–9) points out major differences and similarities between our current world and that of a century ago.

In 1897, vast swathes of land were coloured red: the British empire was at its height. The British were embroiled in a 'scramble for Africa' with other imperial powers, notably France and Germany. Today, by contrast, Britain has turned into a second-division political power. Imperialism is now a dirty word, and the empires themselves are in shards.

In economics, the differences between 1897 and 1997 are, if anything, more striking still. Materially, the world as a whole is far richer: the United States' GDP per head, adjusted for inflation, is more than five times as big as it was 100 years ago; even poor India has seen its GDP per head double.

A close examination of the state of affairs in 1897 from a slightly different angle, however, reveals some interesting similarities too. Now as then, there is one undisputed superpower. Then it was imperial Britain;

in 1997, although it has no territorial empire, it is the United States. The challenges facing the two look similar. Britain's position a century ago seemed unassailable at first glance: it had colonies everywhere, plus ships and naval bases aplenty to defend them. Yet there was a rising threat from Germany. The Germans had their own imperial ambitions, which, with rapid industrialisation, they could begin to afford. Germany's merchant and naval fleets were growing rapidly.

Today the United States' position seems similarly unchallengeable. The only other military superpower since the Second World War, the Soviet Union, has collapsed, and its main successor state, Russia, is weak. The rising economic power of the postwar period, Japan, is constitutionally barred from military adventures. Yet there is one country which could challenge American might in the early twenty-first century in the way that Germany did Britain's in the early twentieth: China. It is already a huge economy, and is quickly becoming a richer one. It has territorial claims over Taiwan and the Spratly Islands. The richest ten nations in our time are more or less the same as they were a century ago, as Table 1.3 shows.

Going back to history again, the benefits derived from the inventions in manufacturing techniques and increased international trade were virtually confined to the industrialised and industrialising nations of the period which followed the Industrial Revolution to our own time. Western Europe and later the United States had as a result a comparative advantage in technology over the rest of the world at the time that some of the great civilisations of the ancient world were in the grip of

Table 1.3   Richest ten nations in the twentieth century

1897	1996
Britain	United States
New Zealand	Norway
United States	Hong Kong
Netherlands	Switzerland
Australia	Denmark
Switzerland	Japan
Belgium	Netherlands
Germany	Singapore
Argentina	France
Denmark	Austria

Source: Adapted from *The Economist*, 20 December 1997.

hibernation and stagnation. There was virtually nothing left of the great-
ness of great nations such as India, Persia, Egypt and China, except
perhaps their visual arts, music, poetry and literature, which were
hardly known beyond their national boundaries.

Even when these and other less economically-advanced nations
emerged into the modern age and started their own industrial revolu-
tions they had further disadvantages in the technological sphere. Some
of the modern technologies and techniques that they had imported
from the more advanced nations were not appropriate to their climatic
and sociocultural conditions. Even today, some of the sophisticated
machinery that is imported to the less-advanced countries does not
work there properly. There is, for instance, a shortage of skilled manpower to operate it or to maintain it when there is a breakdown. This is
directly related to the inadequate educational provisions in some of
these nations, which not only prevent them from understanding and
operating properly the imported technology, but also prevent them
from initiating scientific and technological break-throughs in the first
place. More on this later.

As a result, advanced countries became specialised in manufactured
goods and later in technologically-driven services, such as finance and
insurance. The less-developed nations specialised in primary products
and those business activities which did not require advanced and
sophisticated technology, such as carpet weaving and batik printing.
The characteristics of the market, such as supply, demand and price
fluctuations for agricultural produce and unsophisticated products are
such that the producers have relatively little control over them. In
addition, the value-added element in their finished products is very
small. By contrast, the producers of sophisticated products and services, with higher value-added components, enjoy a much greater
control over their markets. The disadvantages and handicaps suffered
by the former in the international market in comparison with the latter
are obvious.

Industrialised countries, especially the empire builders of the eighteenth and nineteenth centuries, also had other advantages over the less-
powerful nations. The colonies provided them with the supply of cheap
or even free raw materials and captive markets for their manufactured
goods. The international political clout of these countries meant that
they also dominated the international economic and trade scene. They
could and did dictate trade terms. It is not surprising that Britain, the
first nation to industrialise, advocated free trade with other nations
most of which were in no position to compete with her on equal terms.

India, for instance, was a colony and unable to pursue an independent tariff policy. Under British political control during the first half of the nineteenth century, the trade regulations that were imposed on India would probably not have been allowed had the Indian government been independent. As a consequence of these regulations, the imports of cotton goods from Britain increased massively to become the largest category of imports, while cotton piece goods, formerly a major export, dwindled into insignificance (Chaudhuri, 1971; Maddison, 1971).

The slave trade, engaged in officially until the early nineteenth century, and unofficially thereafter for a long time, provided free, strong, able-bodied black labourers for the plantations owned by white settlers in the Americas. True, slavery in Africa, as Reader (1997) points out, did not begin with marauding white men plundering the people from the coasts of West Africa; it was indigenous. Reader exposes the myth that before the arrival of outsiders Africa was a pastoral paradise. But it is also true that Africa was deprived of the fruits of labour of its young men and women in whom it had invested.

In addition to hurting Africa, the white settlers gained a comparative advantage in such commodities as cotton, sugar and coffee over traditional Asian and African growers who had to pay wages to their workers.

The dawn of the twentieth century saw the beginning of the decline of British economic and then political power, as the United States and some western European nations such as Germany and France who had embarked on their industrialisation half a century earlier became formidable competitors in the international marketplace. The loss of her empire, starting with India's independence, completed Britain's process of relegation to a middle-ranking power position. By the end of the Second World War the USA had firmly established its position as an economic and political superpower. Although much of the United States' trade was within the various regions of the country itself, and therefore she participated in international trade proportionately less than other industrialised nations, the rapid growth and sheer size of the economy nevertheless meant that the overall impact of the United States on the international economy was immense (Foreman-Peck, 1983).

In the first half of the twentieth century, two world wars and other cross-border conflicts devastated Europe and redrew its map many times over. By the end of the Second World War, Germany's economy and much of its infrastructure and industrial base were in ruins; those of France were not in any better position thanks to her being occupied by the Nazis and also through the Allied forces' tactical destruction of its infrastructure. The two countries had to start from scratch, with the help of the Marshall Plan, but also more importantly thanks to their own in-built resilience and sheer determination to succeed.

By the 1950s a new and fierce competitor, Japan, began to make its presence felt in the world of international business. It had started its industrialisation process in the previous century and by the beginning of the Second World War had an established industrial base in place. Its economic take-off took a spectacular turn mainly after the Second World War. Some writers on Japan trace the origins of this take-off to the period during which the country was occupied by the USA and was forced to democratise its political system and industrial relations and reform its economic structure and educational system (see for example Locke, 1996). For instance, the Americans dismantled Japan's *zaibatsu* families of companies. One aim of this process was to eliminate producer monopolies that had been so much a part of the prewar Japanese economy. (Later, when the occupation forces left the country the *zaibatsu* was of course replaced by *keiretsu* groups with no apparent damage to the country's competitiveness.) But there were also cultural reasons for Japan's postwar sharp economic rise. The country had suffered humiliation and a spectacular defeat in the Second World War, which for a culture that attaches immense significance to loss of face (Briggs, 1988; Tayeb, 1990) could be buried and forgotten only under an equally spectacular victory, this time on the economic front.

The Soviet bloc which rose to its peak of power after the Second World War and kept its position until its downfall in1989 had its origins in Russia's 1917 revolution, led by Lenin. But it was only after the war that communism swept through a large number of countries, either through revolution and a coup d'etat from within (for example China and Cuba), or through invasion by the Soviet Union (for example eastern and central European countries). The Soviet Union treated its satellite countries as its own property, plundered their natural resources, and polluted their air, water and land with the toxic fumes and wastes of its steel, chemicals and armament industries. Furthermore, the Soviet Union crushed, indirectly through puppet regimes, or directly through military actions, any democratic and human rights movement which rose up in those countries to challenge the Soviet Union's activities in their homeland.

With the coming to power of Mikhail Gorbachev in the Soviet Union in the mid-1980s, a new political and economic era dawned in the Eastern bloc as well as the Soviet Union itself. Within a few years, the central and eastern European countries had gained their political and economic independence and the Soviet Union itself had disintegrated into its constituent republics. Communism, on the face of it, was dead and buried in that part of the world. However, as Child and Czeglédy (1996) point out, it is important to recognise that this transformation has not proceeded uniformly across the countries of eastern Europe. Each has pursued its own path to economic and political reform, and the result is a considerable diversity between the countries in terms of the 'transition indicators'.

The Czech Republic, Hungary, Poland, Slovakia and Slovenia have made the most extensive internal changes and developed the strongest economic relations with western nations. They have high levels of industrialisation and urbanisation, the latter reaching 75 per cent in former Czechoslovakia and around 66 per cent in Hungary and Poland (Economist Intelligence Unit, 1992). They have had the economic resources and infrastructures to effect a rapid transformation away from former socialist institutions, subject to being able to effect the organisational and social changes which are assumed to be necessary. They have been assisted in this latter respect by their historical, cultural and geographical propinquity with neighbouring European countries (particularly Austria, Germany and Scandinavia), and by the advanced level of social and economic development that they had achieved before the imposition of state socialism, compared with other eastern European countries (*The Economist*, 18 November 1995; Child and Czeglédy, 1996).

CULTURE AND NATIONAL COMPETITIVENESS

Fads and fashions ebb and flow in the international business literature much the same as in all other aspects of life. When Japan and other Southeast Asian nations astounded western observers by their economic 'miracles', many quickly offered these nations' peculiar cultures as an explanation. Later, their financial and economic crises in the late 1990s brought out a profusion of explanations, in the confusion of which culture was denounced as irrelevant to the whole affair in both good and bad times (Seizaburo, 1997; *Time Magazine*, 2 February 1998, pp. 56–8; *The Economist*, 25 July 1998, pp. 25–7; Patten, 1998). The present author firmly believes that national culture plays a significant but not a monopolistic role in a country's competitiveness. After all, a government's trade policies and its handling of banking and other financial affairs, its utilisation of advanced technology, education of people, and legal and other institutional infrastructure do not exist in a vacuum. This section consequently intends to further examine the role of national culture.

Religions in many countries, with either secular or religious constitutions, have a certain degree of influence on the cultural characteristics of their people and their institutions. So let us start with the religion of the nation which was the first to industrialise and achieved competitive advantage over its counterparts at the time – Britain. The main religion of the British is Christianity, with the adherents of various Protestant denominations forming by far the largest proportion of the population as a whole. Protestantism was initiated by Luther in Germany in the early sixteenth century and expanded by Calvin in Switzerland. It came to England during the reign of Henry VIII and later expanded to other parts of the country. Protestantism, as part of its protest against the interposition of the Church between God and the believer, tended to replace the patterns of the society in which the institutions of the Church were integrated with a more individualistic system.

For Weber (1930) the change of the economic structure in England from feudalism to capitalism and private ownership occurred in the sixteenth century. One of the contributory factors, according to Weber, was the peculiar 'ethic' which stressed untiring, never-ending acquisition which developed in certain parts of Protestant Europe. It is well-known that Weber believed that this ethic was somehow associated with Calvinism though not in any simple system of cause and effect. In Weber's view, Protestantism stood at the cradle of modern economic man, and Calvinism in particular stressed the individual, one's own ability and initiative. Thus, though modern western capitalism 'was derived from the peculiarities of the social structure of Occident, it was inconceivable without Calvinism' (p. 25) , for it 'had the psychological effect of freeing the acquisition of goods from the inhibitions of traditionalistic ethics' (p. 171).

According to Weber, Christianity was one of the factors which broke the original 'clan' system in Europe. It encouraged an abstract, non-familistic attitude, and stressed individual behaviour; every Christian community was basically a confessional association of individual believers, not a ritual association of kinship groups. While Christianity in general was dissolvent of the earlier State, Protestantism was especially more powerful in its attack on the 'fetters' of earlier kinship systems. Weber argued that the great achievement of ethical religions, above all of the ethical and asceticist sects of Protestantism, was to shatter the fetters of the kinship group. These religions established the superior community of faith of a common ethical way of life in opposition to the community of blood, even to a large extent in opposition to the family. It is however true to say that the origins of individualism and the 'capitalist ethic' in England lay well before the sixteenth century (McFarlane, 1978). It seems, at any rate, that Protestantism, since its adoption by the English, has encouraged and reinforced individualism and the spirit of capitalism in the society.

The role of the Protestant ethic in the economic advancement of Britain and other Protestant nations does not of course mean that it is the only religion in the world whose followers can prosper economically, or that only western civilisations can achieve economic and business excellence. Like many other aspects of life, there are more ways than one to achieve the same end. As West (1989, p. 5) puts it, 'Southeast Asian cultures have turned on its head the long-held claim that successful modernisation was somehow linked to the "particularistic" values associated with Western thought'.

The present author disagrees totally with Huntington (1993, 1996), who, somewhat patronisingly, argues that western ideas of individualism, liberalism, constitutionalism, human rights, equality, liberty, the rule of law, democracy, free markets and the separation of church and state, often have little resonance in Islamic, Confucian, Japanese, Hindu, Buddhist or Orthodox cultures. Until recently most western countries did not enjoy these western ideas, these 'fruits of Western civilisation'. These ideas are products of modern industrial civilisation rather than classical western civilisation, widely shared across many cultures, and have had to be fought for in the West as anywhere else (see also Seizaburo, 1997, and a special survey on Human Rights in *The Economist*, 5 December 1998). Moreover, other religions are not devoid of similar values as Christianity which, having originated in the East, has come to symbolise the western civilisation.

Islam, for instance, has always encouraged its believers to engage in commerce and private enterprise. Mohammed, the Muslims' prophet, as a young man worked for a woman trader/merchant whom he subsequently married. Many of the values espoused by Islam, if followed to the letter, are conducive to success in business and commerce: individual responsibility within a framework of cooperation with others; fatalism but also a recognition of personal choice; work ethic and individualism/self-reliance; patience; self-discipline and abstinence; resolve; sincerity, truthfulness and trust. Indonesia, Malaysia and Turkey will probably be the first predominantly Muslim countries to achieve true industrialisation without depending on oil and other underground resources.

India, where Hinduism's caste system remains deeply ingrained, is showing new signs of growth. True, this is in part a result of her shift from a policy of protecting domestic industries by import substitution to a policy of economic development through liberalisation and export promotion. But it is also true that Hinduism does not pose an obstacle to industrialisation and economic advancement.

Confucianism, a much debated creed nowadays, is characterised by family and group orientation, respect for age and hierarchy, a preference for harmony and avoidance of conflict and of competition, thrift and conservatism in social mores. These values greatly differ from those of Protestant and other Christian nations, but have nevertheless helped create a culture which has served as the backdrop of economic success. The four Asian tigers, some of whose population subscribe to Confucianism or similar creeds, have a highly skilled, committed and loyal workforce who are prepared to sacrifice themselves for the good of their company to a far greater extent than are their counterparts in some other nations. As industrialists, these nations are very entrepreneurial, aggressive and competitive, just like their Protestant and individualist counterparts in the West.

An important point to note here is that most religions practised around the world are far from monolithic and come in many flavours, from fundamentalist to secular, including strands that have championed rationality, free market and scientific inquiry. Take Islam for example (Tayeb, 1997). Although Muslim nations have a great deal in common, there are also differences among them; and these differences can be observed in economic and business as well as social aspects of life. Saudi Arabia, for instance, adheres strictly to the Sacred law (Shari'a) in many spheres of life, while Turkey has turned to secular laws for the administration of its economic and social affairs. The position of women in society and in business life, and the socially acceptable code of behaviour for people in general, provide some illustrations in this regard.

The *Taliban* regime in Afghanistan, especially in the urban and rural areas under its control, does not allow women to work outside their homes or girls to attend schools and other educational institutions. The authorities have even ordered windows of all houses to be painted over so that unveiled women cannot be seen from outside. A woman's face is considered to be a cause of men's corruption and therefore has to be covered. Men are told to grow beards.

In Pakistan in the early 1980s, General Zia Islamised the country's law and introduced new codes of conduct. For instance, government employees had to give up their European-style clothing and adhere to strict Islamic dress. Education in state schools was segregated, and girls were required to wear head scarves. The economy was to be run on Islamic lines, including reinstitution of an old Islamic wealth tax, *zakat*, and Islamic banking practices. Many of General Zia's Islamic laws are still in force in the country. In 1998 a new Shari'a Law further entrenched Islamic rules in the country's statutory book.

In Malaysia the government, as discussed in a later chapter, has been implementing an Islamisation policy for sometime now, according to which companies have to organise their activities and manage their employees in accordance with Koranic teachings. The chief Minister of the State of Kelantan has taken this further (*The Economist*, 26 October 1996). The market by the bus station in the state capital looks similar to others in Malaysia: it is filled with stalls selling satay, noodles, fruit and pancakes. But at sunset the market empties, the food is covered and the hungry are expelled by guards with megaphones, until, 20 minutes later, the mosque disgorges the faithful after prayers. In supermarkets, separate checkout queues have been instituted for men and women. Unisex hairdressers are banned. Most recently, women have been warned not to wear 'excessive lipstick'.

In Turkey, the balance between secular and religious, having been tilted sharply in a secular direction by Ataturk in the 1920s and 1930s, has now shifted back towards Islam. Religious education is much more widespread than it used to be. More women now wear a mild form of the garb prescribed by Islamic modesty. In the 1995 general elections an Islamic party won 20 per cent of the vote, the largest share for a single party. This party has promised to take Turkey back into the centre of the Islamic world.

In Saudi Arabia, women are not allowed to drive their own cars; and as far as work is concerned, they are barred from public office. As a result, they have turned to business and the professions for employment. But here, too, they work under certain constraints. According to *The Economist* (4 February 1995) most women who are active in private businesses (as owners) are in the retail trade: in a shopping mall in Jeddah, eight out of 20 shops are owned and run by women and notices forbid men to enter the shops women run. Teaching is a profession open to women but it is difficult for them to apply for positions which are located outside their home towns. In this patriarchal society, women must have written permission from their husbands or fathers before they can travel. Women generally operate under difficulties: they have to be discreet, and the places where they work are segregated.

In Iran women have to follow a strict Islamic dress code at work, and indeed elsewhere. A policy of segregation of sexes is observed in prayers, at wedding ceremonies, on public transport, in queues at shops and so forth. However, unlike Arab women in Saudi Arabia and the Persian Gulf states, Iranian women are doing well in many spheres of public life. Some 95 per cent of young girls go to primary school. Older girls have a smaller chance than boys of getting higher education, but the gap is closing. They are doing well in technical schools, colleges and universities. Women can enter most jobs and professions, and, unlike their Saudi counterparts, they can drive their cars and vote. They can stand for parliament and there are many women members of parliament.

In Kazakhistan, under the USSR culture, women could and did achieve high positions in business. Now that the country is independent, its old, predominantly patriarchal culture which lay dormant under Soviet rule is enjoying a revival, replacing the 'Russian communist' culture. As a result, the perception of the role of women in society and in the workplace is changing.

It is also worth noting that religion, like much else in society, can be used as a political tool to manipulate the public's values, opinions and actions, and in the process, perhaps unwittingly, may impact on their economic as well as political activities. The policy of the Taliban's regime in Afganistan to forbid girls and women to become educated and to work has nothing to do with the true Islamic values and precepts as handed down through the centuries from Mohammed and his followers. The suppression of scientific inquiry and freedom of intellectual pursuits by the Christian church in Europe through much of the Middle Ages was a grotesque distortion of that religion whose origins lay in tolerance of contrasting views and thinking. It is, in other words, the distorted religions in certain countries which are holding back their people from realising their potentials in economic as well as other spheres of life.

There are of course other sources and originators of national culture besides religion, such as ecology, family structure and relationships (see for instance, Hofstede, 1980; Tayeb, 1996a), some of which might enhance the influence of religion on the national make up and others which might balance it out. It is not an accident of history, for example, that North Americans are one of the most individualistic, assertive, entrepreneurial and at the same time successful nations in business terms. The white settlers, which make up the vast majority of the population, are descendants of the people who left the 'old world' over five hundred years ago, with barely a worldly possession to their name, in search of new horizons and opportunities, a feat not for the faint hearted.

In a recent publication, Reader (1997) explains much of Africa's history by its fragile soils and erratic weather. They make for conservative social and political systems. He argues that the communities which endured were those that directed available energies primarily towards minimising the risk of failure, not maximising returns. This created societies designed for survival, not development; the qualities needed for survival are the opposite of those needed for developing, that is making experiments and taking risks. Some societies were wealthy, but accumulating wealth was next to impossible; most people bartered and there were few traders. Everybody had to keep moving. Africans were nomads or pastoralists or farmers constantly shifting as land became exhausted. This is why experience of the past was all-important and why gerontocracy became, one way or another, Africa's political system. Its societies were organised in age-sets in which the eldest ruled. They still do: few of Africa's leaders are under 60, well above the average life expectancy.

Landes (1998) analysing the processes of economic evolution in various parts of the world, especially Europe, argues that natural endowments (a temperate climate, adequate water, the absence of virulent disease) gave some areas of the world, notably Europe, an enormous economic advantage. But European exceptionalism went beyond climate. Unlike Islamic or eastern societies, Europe made a distinction between the secular and the religious, had decentralised authority, and placed far greater emphasis on private property rights. All this promoted a culture of inventiveness that set Europe on a very different path from other civilisations.

EDUCATION AND NATIONAL COMPETITIVENESS

Education plays a significant role in modern societies in that, among other things, it determines the quality of their human resources. A comparison between the educational systems of some of the internationally competitive countries with those of some non-runners provides an interesting picture.

India is proud of its achievements in education. It has many excellent universities, and one of the biggest stocks of technically trained manpower in the world. However, the country as a whole has a very low literacy rate in comparison with the Asian tigers or even her fellow developing nation, Iran (see Table 1.1 above). Whereas India's spending has been lavish on universities, in East Asia the emphasis has been on teaching the basics to all children. In the early stages of industrialisation the Asian tigers poured educational resources into primary and secondary education rather than higher education. This has helped them to increase the productivity of the mass of the workforce, which is what counts in an *industrialising* country whose comparative advantage will temporarily be light manufacturing.

Many nations, from Japan to Iran, in the early stages of their industrialisation searched for educational models in the West, notably the United States, either by design or under occupation. However, some countries realised very early that those models either needed modifications to suit their own socioeconomic circumstances or had to be discarded altogether. But some others have adopted these models uncritically and as a result failed to prepare their people to embark on the process of industrialisation with competence and confidence.

Locke (1996) lucidly explains why the MBA taught-course never caught on in postwar German management education. The Germans examined American management teaching models and then, having discarded them, decided to do 'something else', a 'scientific' model which aims at the schooling of the mind. The system does not make people 'job ready' but 'job able'. In other words, it does not pretend to train people to manage, as American MBA courses do, but helps them to become capable of managing. In Japan, again, Locke explains how no American-style management education of the MBA type materialised, in spite of the educational reforms introduced in the country under the occupation. Unlike the American system, the Japanese model emphasises process- as well as result-orientation, group-work, a sense of duty and a generalist approach to acquiring knowledge and skills – a model which suits their own cultural heritage. As Locke (1996) argues, 'the Japanese refusal to . . . reform their educational structures in ways that would accommodate the needs of an American style of managerialism, marks the limits of American influence' (p. 143).

This is in sharp contrast to Iran's management education policies, not only when she was under the political influence of the United States before the 1979 revolution, but also after that influence disappeared completely. Iran benefits from a growing army of educated managers with MBA and other business degrees from home and abroad, in addition to a large number of managers and executives who have higher degrees in other disciplines (Amirshahi, unpublished manuscript). However, many of the MBA and business degree holders have probably not received the kind of education which would be needed to operate successfully in the current Iranian economy, as Latifi (1997) found in her study.

Latifi's research exposed the gap between Iranian managers' professional and skill needs and what is on offer in universities and business schools. MBA courses, for instance, are generally modelled after American and European ones, which are primarily designed for their own domestic needs. Marketing and financial accounting classes, for example, are intended for managers working in an open-door capitalist market with a vibrant private sector and widespread public share-ownership, sophisticated consumers, easily accessible economic and demographic data, and so forth. The appropriateness of such courses for managers working in a protected economy dominated by the public sector is rather doubtful. In fact the mangers who participated in Latifi's study considered such courses as irrelevant.

THE ROLE OF THE STATE

An important manifestation of culture at the macro level is the extent to which the state is regarded by society as a whole as having an important role in managing and directing economic activities. Anglo-Americans, for example, have traditionally viewed the state's role as the upholder of law and order and the defender of national security. It is regarded, in the US more so than in Britain, at best as an enabler and at worst as a nuisance as far as the economy and trade policies are concerned. The trend in Britain, which had many nationalised industries until the late 1970s, was in the subsequent two decades or so to hand over many of the state-owned enterprises to the private sector. In other equally or more competitive nations such as France, Japan and certain Southeast Asian countries, by contrast, the state has always played a crucial role not only in the overall management of the economy, but also in the ownership and management of industries.

However, both in the United States and Britain governments have intervened in the economy in varying degrees at different times. In the USA, for example, as Lall (1996) points out, the government has played a significant role at both micro and macro levels of economic and industrial policies, such as human capital formation, technology investment and corporate strategies, exchange rates and interest rates on which the country's competitiveness *vis-à-vis* other leading developed nations depends. Moreover both at early and recent stages of development of industrial competitiveness the government has a larger role to play through such interventions as infant industry protection, infrastructure development, procurement, education and R&D (directly through its space and defence programmes).

Japan clearly and purposefully directed its economy on its way to industrialisation. By creating a competitive domestic market in which inefficient industries died and the more competitive ones flourished the government provided an environment in which major Japanese companies were trained to beat foreign competitors when they later ventured abroad. At the same time the state sheltered its domestic companies from foreign competition for decades while they were finding their feet on firm ground. The government's interventions have not of course always been helpful, as witnessed in the financial crisis of the late 1990s.

In the so-called Asian tigers, too, governments managed economic development and the industrialisation process. Taiwan, for instance, had one of the largest public enterprise sectors outside the communist bloc and sub-Saharan Africa from the 1950s to the 1970s (Wade, 1990). According to Whitley (1992), state support and connections are often a crucial aspect of business activities in Southeast Asian societies, particularly in South Korea (Amsden, 1989; Jones and Sakong, 1980), and form a key component of their dominant business systems. This support does not, though, usually extend to the granting of monopoly powers or toleration of sustained inefficiency. Rather, it tends to reward success and punish failure and so 'accelerate market forces' (Abegglen and Stalk, 1985 pp. 136–44). The Taiwanese state has pursued 'developmentalist' policies, in the sense that it has systematically encouraged industrialisation and export sectors since the 1950s (Cumings, 1987; Gold, 1988; Haggard, 1988). Tax incentives and selective assistance for exporters have directed entrepreneurs' attention to particular sectors, such as plastics and electronics (Amsden, 1985; Hamilton, 1989; Orru, 1991), and the state has tended to use public enterprises as the preferred instrument for sector development (Whitley, 1992).

In South Korea, primarily through credit rationing and control of the banking system, but also through the tax system, control over licences and other administrative devices, state agencies have exercised decisive influence on the strategic choices and investment decisions of the favoured conglomerates, or *chaebol* (Amsden, 1989; Jones and Sakong, 1980; Kim, 1988; Wade, 1990). The oligopolistic pattern of industrial structure in many heavy manufacturing industries is largely the result of state coordination of economic activities and encouragement of particular developments (Whitley, 1992). Through cheap loans and other inducements certain *chaebol* have been pushed into new sectors of activity, while others have been discouraged from entering these areas (Zeile, 1989). Generally, as Whitley (1992) points out, the state ensured that at least two *chaebol* had firms in each of the new industries it wanted to develop but restricted the total number to ensure significant profits and opportunities for expansion.

China's leaders have also looked to Southeast Asia's state-directed capitalisms as proof that capitalist economic tools could be operated safely with strong central control. In 1997 China announced that thousands of small state-owned firms would soon be freed to take their chances in a 'socialist' marketplace. Some hinted that eventually the 1000 or so largest firms might be reorganised into South Korean-style *chaebol* (*The Economist*, 4 February 1998).

In France, under both Socialist and Gaulist governments, the state has always maintained an active role in the economy. French politicians, especially those of socialist persuasions, prefer a social market economy to a more *laissez-faire*, unfettered capitalism advocated and practised by their American counterparts. Prime Minister Lionel Jospin, in an interview in 1998, said that with regard to the subject of the sale of state assets 'my approach is simple. When something is being done well, there is no need for change.' He then defended keeping in public hands utilities and other monopolies that play a role in ensuring the fair provision of essential services across the country, and said 'I think the market should be tempered'. He further added, 'I know my country well, an enforced conversion to ultra liberalism would just not work' (*Voyager*, July/August, 1998, pp. 57–63).

In developing countries such as Iran and India, governments have always played a dominant role in the economy, as we shall see in Chapter 2. Moreover, because of the security that government jobs carry in these countries, ordinary people actually prefer a job in state-owned enterprises as well as various ministries and departments.

SUMMARY

This chapter has evaluated the economic and non-economic well-being of a number of countries using various criteria, from GDP growth rate to life expectancy in order to explore some of the major socio-political explanations for their success and failure in achieving competitive status in the world.

It has been argued that for a nation to be competitive it is not sufficient merely to have ample supply of resources such as minerals, oil, rain forests and human resources; rather, it is the way in which these resources are managed and utilised which makes all the difference. Culture and culture-building institutions, such as religion and education play significant roles here. Certain cultural values and attitudes, such as entrepreneurial drive and a work ethic, were argued to lie in part behind the competitiveness of a nation, with their absence depriving it of competitiveness. In addition, there are culture-building institutions, such as education and religion, which not only inculcate these and other values in people but also help train and prepare them for contributions to their country's performance. It is believed that most religions are quite capable of building up in their followers the values and attitudes necessary for success in business. But, in practice, and for mainly political reasons, many religious doctrines and precepts have been distorted to the extent that they have, at times and in places, had quite the opposite effect.

The chapter has also presented a broad-brush view of the major historical roots of success and failure of nations. Industrial revolution, colonialisation, slavery, scientific breakthrough and technological innovations in the past three centuries or so allowed certain countries to gain the upper hand in the political and economic arena, while some superpowers of times past lost their economic and political advantages as they failed to maintain sovereignty over their affairs and, among other things, to catch up with the latest scientific and technological developments. The role of the state in the economy has also been discussed and the ways in which this role is discharged. Chapter 2 will take up this point again and elaborate on it further.

2 Nations as Launch Pads for Internationalisation

INTRODUCTION

It has been argued by some commentators (see for instance Lehmann, 1998) that in all industrialised countries, irrespective of their 'capitalist system', there has in the recent past been an increasing divergence between companies and countries. This line of argument means that the fortunes of a country's firms, especially those with international interests and activities, are independent of their country of origins. For example, in the late 1990s the deep travails in which the Japanese economy found itself did not mean that the demise of leading Japanese corporations was nigh. The global dynamism and success of Canon, Hoya, Honda, Toyota, TDK, Rohm and Sony, known as the 'seven samurai', contrasted with the quagmire of the Japanese economy. Similarly, the future prospects of the Charoen Pokphand Group, the Salim Group and Sime Darby are not exclusively dependent on the future prospects of their countries of origin, respectively Thailand, Indonesia and Malaysia.

The present author argues, however, that while the above examples might indeed indicate a degree of decoupling of national and company fortunes, this is not the whole picture. It is, for instance, inconceivable that domestic companies in the countries which are still in the early stages of industrialisation and which are encumbered with serious infrastructural inadequacies become international competitors, despite a few rare exceptions. A vast majority of companies need a home-base helping hand to get to a stage where they can decouple themselves from that aid. Japanese, German, American and British competitive companies may now be independent of their home country, but they could not have got where they are without a solid launching platform in the first place.

Many nations are both homes and hosts to international firms. As hosts, they can adopt certain policies, based on their overall political-economic priorities, which aim to attract foreign firms. The appeal of lucrative returns due to market size, growth prospects, cost of labour and other factors could bring in foreign direct investment which in turn could have implications for the host nations' level of employment, technological advancement, increased competition in the domestic market and even culture, on a superficial level at least. As homes to international firms, nations provide many opportunities, as discussed in Chapter 1, which if exploited can stand them in good stead. In other words, as companies go about the world competing with others to gain market share, countries are competing to retain and/or increase their share of both domestic and foreign investment. In addition, the efforts of governments are directed not only at seeking to get foreign companies to come in, but at preventing native companies going out, lock stock and barrel.

In recent years, the intensification of international competition has led to a growing preoccupation with determinants of competitiveness. Interest is increasingly focused on issues related to productivity and technical change. There is a healthy debate between those who advocate deregulation, competition and non-interventions, and those who recognise a role for government policies in the matter in order to ensure that firms do not develop a tendency towards lock-in, whereby long-term technical development and innovation are endangered.

As Michie and Prendergast (1997) argue, without competition there is no reason to change, but, paradoxically, an excessive emphasis on market-type flexibility can lock firms and industries into existing products and routines of production. Once lock-in occurs, very substantial reforms may be necessary before development once again becomes possible. In addition, the authors argue, while there is evidence that networks and groups of firms can increase the scope for innovation, they do not always do so. The problems may be due to coordination failure and /or capability failure. As an example of the former the authors cite the Taiwanese electronics industry. In the main, the industry is made up of small and medium-sized enterprises which concentrate almost exclusively on the manufacturing function to the neglect of areas such as marketing and R&D which are necessary for the upgrading of their technological level (Gee, 1993; Chou, 1995). As a result, the role of state has been extremely important in building competence in advanced electronics, with leadership of the industry vested in public sector research organisations and public enterprise (Wade, 1990).

By contrast, in the Japanese case, intervention is mainly aimed at facilitating the creation of convergent technological expectations, thereby reducing risk but also leaving a good deal of space for competition among technologically leading firms (Wade, 1990; Porter, 1990).

In line with Howells and Michie (1997), it is argued here that the competitive advantage of firms and of the economies from which they operate is built up by conscious policy actions by firms, governments and others. It is not determined by some sort of natural, resource endowment-determined comparative advantage. And as the economy becomes more globalised, any competitive advantage gained (or lost) will have that much greater effect on market share, output, employment levels and living standards. Thus, far from being swept aside by forces such as technological globalisation, economic and industrial policy is becoming more, not less, important in building a suitable launching pad for a nation's firms to engage successfully in international business.

The present chapter focuses on national governments' trade policies, including policies regarding membership of regional agreements, as one of the important means which provide such platforms for home-grown companies as well as the competitiveness of the country itself.

POLITICAL ECONOMIC POLICIES IN RECENT TIMES AND THEIR IMPLICATIONS FOR NATIONAL COMPETITIVENESS

Everywhere, with a few notable exceptions, the general trend of economic and trade policies in the last two decades of the twentieth century has been towards liberalisation, deregulation, privatisation and 'small government', a trend which is set to continue into the twenty-first century, Henderson's (1999) objection to such a proposition notwithstanding. In the international sphere the liberalising trend has also accelerated, with initiatives such as Europe's single market, NAFTA, and above all the Uruguay Round of GATT talks that gave birth to the WTO. The picture is not of course in every case as clear-cut as this. In most countries some parts of the economy (notably education, health, pensions and labour markets) are still dominated by public provision and/or heavy regulation. But nobody would deny there has been a change of direction. In addition, foreign direct investment has been considered, especially by many developing nations, as a means to increase and maintain their industrialisation drive. The money provided by foreigners, for example, is largely responsible for China's export success. And most recent growth in the economy appears to have come from exports, which rose by over 20 per cent in 1997 (*The Economist*, 14 February 1998).

However, not all these aspiring nations have been either successful in attracting foreign investors or willing to do so. Moreover, there are other aspects of their trade and economic policies which have held them back, if not been downright harmful to their ultimate aim of economic advancement.

Books and articles on international business are filled with discussions of the factors which pull foreigners to a country, or indeed keep successful companies anchored at home – political stability, tax incentives, technological know-how, an educated workforce, raw materials, a flexible labour market, a growing customer base and so forth. Of these factors, the present chapter focuses on the trade policies of a sample of nations as an explanation for their success or otherwise in the international market. In addition, where relevant, references will be made to the infrastructural political economic institutions of these countries, because these, as discussed in Chapter 1, determine the environment in which markets operate. Using data from 94 countries over three decades, a study conducted by the World Bank (*Development Report 1997*) showed that it is not just economic policies and human capital, but the quality of a country's institutions that determines economic outcomes.

Starting with the ex-Soviet bloc, the communists have apparently gone for ever, but their legacy of decades of mismanagement of the economy is proving harder to eradicate. Russia, for example, is suffering from acute institutional problems, especially with respect to legal and taxation systems. It embarked on economic reforms without first having put in place the necessary supporting political and institutional infrastructure. As a result, the reforms themselves have faltered, the economy is blighted by financial crises and infested with the mafia, whose criminal and protection activities have made the country unsafe for foreign investors.

Moreover, by 1998, President Yeltsin, who through various constitutional amendments had managed to concentrate a great deal of power in the president's office, appeared to be no longer 'the master of any game save that of shuffling his ministers and advisers with disruptive frequency' (*The Economist*, 14 February 1998). His lack of commitment and clarity in economic policy helped condemn Russia to a recession far longer and deeper than that of most other transitional economies. Confusing and incoherent economic objectives declared by various senior ministers and officials would lead one only to believe that Russia hardly had an economic policy at all. Russia, judging by its record so far, is far from being a country which can produce successful multinational companies. It has been able to attract some hardy global enterprises, notably from Germany, followed by the United States, Japan and the United Kingdom, but it is nowhere near some of its fellow ex-communist countries of central and eastern Europe.

Poland, Hungary and the Czech Republic have been far more successful in stabilising their economies. Poland adopted a shock therapy approach, and suffered initially from high inflation rates, mass unemployment and poverty while it embarked on a course of privatisation and treatment for its chronic over-manning problems. Hungary had already, well before the 1989 revolution, had a reasonably large private sector and its economy was more prepared than others to embrace a capitalist model. These two together with the Czech Republic have been actively seeking, and receiving, foreign investment, mainly in joint venture forms. This policy has helped bring in advanced technological know-how that thanks to the international politics of the Cold War era they were deprived of. All three countries had a highly educated workforce, but they needed retraining to learn new skills, such as operating modern technology. They had to rebuild their legal base and taxation systems, which they had decades ago, but which were deformed or eliminated under communism.

The picture in these countries, however, is far from rosy. Hungary, for example, made good progress in the initial years of transformation, but the reform process slowed in 1993–4, and by 1994 the privatisation of state firms had ground to a halt while both the budget and current account deficits soared to unsustainable levels. The situation improved in 1995 and the privatisation effort was renewed later in the year.

But these nations have adopted trade and other economic policies which are bound to strengthen their position in the international market and make them competitive players sooner or later. The Czech Republic, for instance, is viewed by western observers as one of the most politically and economically stable post-communist states. Its key macroeconomic indicators are, in the aggregate, the best in the region, and public opinion polls show a strong support for reform. Inflation and unemployment of 8.7 per cent and 3.3 per cent respectively in 1996 are among the lowest in the region. Prague's mass privatisation programme, including its innovative distribution of ownership shares to Czech citizens via 'coupon vouchers', has made the most rapid progress in eastern Europe. About 80 per cent of the economy is in private hands or is partially privatised. Such a situation is far from being within the reach of India and Iran – two nations which were the cradles of great civilisations, and in the case of the latter a powerful empire, in the times past. They could both have been central and western Asia's tigers but they have missed the opportunity so far.

India gained its independence from Britain roughly at the same time that central and eastern European nations lost theirs to the Soviet Union. Since 1989 these European countries have achieved far more in terms of economic advancement than has India in the past 50 years, thanks mainly to their respective trade and other economic policies. India, like many other developing countries which were until a few decades ago the colonies of major imperial powers, is suspicious of foreign powers and intends to avoid domination at all cost. For this reason, she considers self-reliance, economic growth and industrialisation as her top priorities, and is willing to sacrifice everything to achieve them. But has India been successful in achieving its goals? The answer seems to be an emphatic no. India has not achieved the level and growth rate of per capita output that its endowments of productive inputs and institutions would seem to warrant (Trinque, 1993).

Since independence in 1947, successive governments in India have pursued semi-socialist and protectionist industrial and economic policies. The private sector has been allowed to operate, in a strictly regulated market, side by side with the state-owned enterprises. Like many other third-world countries, the government has played an active role in the management of the economy, with several objectives: eradication of poverty, industrialisation of the economy, creation of employment, redistribution of wealth, and, ultimately, economic self-reliance. In practice, however, many of these objectives have not been achieved. Massive poverty, inequality between the rich and poor, a high level of illiteracy and infant mortality are still as pronounced in the country as they were in the late 1940s (Sharma, 1992).

In pursuit of these policies, the government embarked on a series of interventionist five-yearly development plans. These plans, implemented at the micro-levels, amounted to dictating to business firms what, how and where to produce, and at what price to sell their products. The state even interfered with the staffing and other internal policies of the firms. For instance, they were encouraged to employ labour-intensive technologies in order to increase the level of employment, and quotas were set for the companies to recruit workers from among lower castes and migrants from rural areas.

The consequences of a virtually closed and insular economy are enormous, the most serious of which are the neglect of industrial modernisation and the phenomenon of industrial sickness (Johri, 1992). One manifestation of this industrial sickness can be seen in both state-owned and private organisations. The government's enterprises are run with extraordinary inefficiency. Various BICP (India's Bureau of

Industrial Costs and Prices) studies of state-owned steel plants, coal mines, shipyards, machine-tool factories and so on have found the same management failures every time: under-use of capacity, poor materials planning, excessive inventories, egregious over-staffing, obsolete technology, inadequate maintenance and inappropriate products. The costs are simply passed on to India's private sector in the form of either higher prices (especially to private industrial customers) or higher taxes. In the private sector, the restriction on imports and foreign investment, in the name of building up national industries and economic self-reliance, has resulted in coddled, inefficient enterprises which are in no position to compete with the seasoned firms from North America, Western Europe and East Asia.

According to an Indian top trade official, until recently, India was just off the map as far as world trade and investment are concerned. The figures back him up: the world's second most populous nation accounts for less than 0.5 per cent of global commerce (*Time*, 10 January, 1994). IMF figures available from 1950 to 1994 shows a downward trend in the period from just over 2 per cent to just over .05 per cent of world export (*The Economist*, 21 January 1995). The scene is changing gradually and slowly. Since 1991 the government has started a process of limited liberalisation. The reforms have virtually dismantled investment licensing and removed the government controls over private sector firms' investment and production decisions. Although state enterprises are not privatised, a policy of equity dilution is being implemented. That is, some of the shares in these enterprises are available for sale to the private sector. Moreover, private companies are encouraged to invest in the same industries where up until mid-1991 the state held a monopoly position. The liberalisation process has been extended to other economic spheres as well, such as the financial sector and exchange rate regime.

As for foreign trade, the market has been opened up to foreign competition to some extent by removing some of the barriers to foreign investment, and reducing import tariffs (except for consumer goods). Until 1992, for instance, foreign firms were not allowed to control more than 40 per cent of a domestic enterprise; now they may acquire as much as 51 per cent and, with special government permission, even 100 per cent. But the government bureaucracy and the private sector vested interests are slowing the process down.

Businessmen, although understanding the need for liberalisation, seem reluctant, as they have a stake in the present system. The most successful have learned to manipulate the rules and the bureaucrats in charge, and have invested heavily to that end. Moreover, protection means less competition and safe profits. Businessmen may be waking up to what this approach has done to the economy as a whole, but they are bound to fear that they themselves will lose out if real reform ever happens (*The Economist*, 4 May 1991). There is also opposition to the government's economic reform programmes from trade unions and some politicians *(Financial Express*, 20 February, 1992; *Wall Street Journal*, Eastern Edition, 17 January 1994).

Moreover, the general election in 1998 brought to office the Hindu nationalist BJP (Bharatiya Janata Party) which, if any, placed even greater emphasis on the country's protectionism and consequently on international isolation. For example, the Party argued that Indian industry must essentially be built by Indians, and foreign investment can be only a modest supplement, though it has an important role in some areas such as infrastructure. The Party also intended to restrict foreign direct investment in non-priority areas and stop hostile take-overs of Indian companies by foreign ones. In addition, the government's first budget intended to boost growth by increasing public spending, notably on defence, and promote industrial development by raising tariffs, already among the highest in the world, by eight percentage points across the board. These policies are taking India back not merely to the pre-reform era of the 1970s and 1980s but to the Nehruvian model of the 1950s and 1960s – a time, and an approach to develop-ment, that has secured to this day India's place among the poorest countries of the world.

Such protectionist and inward-looking policies would obviously discourage all but the most seasoned foreign investors and multina-tionals. They also prevent the internationalisation of otherwise capable domestic companies who would like to expand their markets beyond India's borders. There is, for instance, little point in seeking to become a global player until the Indian government allows its domestically domiciled corporations full capital-account convertibility. The govern-ment has never freely allowed, and continues to control, the movement of capital overseas to acquire foreign assets.

India, however, has a great potential for future success, according to Thomas (1994). The country has the necessary infrastructure for eco-nomic reforms, such as a large private sector, established financial insti-tutions and stockmarket, well-trained managers, and English as the language of commerce and central administration. This places India in a better position in the international market than say China, where this infrastructure has yet to be established. But the country suffers from its leaders' inability to realise her potentials and make her a star performer on the international stage that she deserves to be (Tayeb, 1996b).

Iran (Tayeb, 1999a) is a developing country which started its process of modernisation and industrialisation nearly a century ago. At some point she even dreamed of becoming the second Japan of Asia. However, the country has had a turbulent time both before and after the 1979 revolution, which resulted in the third change of political regime within the century. In the past 20 years alone the country has undergone drastic political, economic and cultural transformations. The Islamic revolution of 1979, which followed a few years of civil and industrial unrest during the last stage of the Shah's reign, set the scene. The 1980s began with a devastating and debilitating war with Iraq which lasted for eight years and drained the country of its resources, both natural and human, and brought the country's process of economic development and industrialisation to a grinding halt. The war interrupted the export of oil and left much of the country's oil installation and other industries and the infrastructure in ruins. The total damage is estimated at around $400m in addition to some $90bn of the financial costs of military activities.

In addition, because of the changes in the relations between Iran and major western countries there was an almost overnight halt to foreign direct investment which had hitherto provided some of the momentum for economic growth. Later, for one reason or another, sanctions were piled upon sanctions which aggravated these already uneasy relations, and which in turn had serious implications for Iran's economy in general and its foreign trade in particular. Foreign direct investment from non-western countries, especially those in Southeast Asia, was the first to flow slowly in again after the end of the war with Iraq in the late 1980s and has increased gradually since then. In the late 1990s efforts were made, by all sides concerned, to improve relations with western nations, and a few European companies started to develop business interests in the country. However, because of internal political struggles between various factions and certain unease in the relationships between Iran and the USA and the European Union, progress has been very slow on that front.

The Islamic revolution also had other profound implications for the economy and the society as whole. For instance, almost immediately after the new regime was established, all banks were nationalised and foreign participation in the financial sector was removed. Later, in 1984, a law came into effect that was designed to make the banking sector subject to Islamic rules, replacing the payment of interest with profit- and risk-sharing schemes. The system redirects capital away from long-term investment to short-term ventures: this is so because creditors will have to wait until the projects that they finance come to fruition before they can get their share of profits, if any.

The economy, although it is a capitalist one, is run on a strict protectionist and statist model. Many industries and firms, which in a large number of capitalist countries would normally be in private hands, are owned and managed by the state in Iran. It is estimated that the government's share of the ownership of the economy is 80 per cent. The government has tried in recent years to reduce subsidies and price control over certain commodities and food products but the process is inevitably a slow one. Attempts were also made in the early 1990s to reform the economy and start a process of privatisation and open up the economy to foreign investment, but the programme faltered, mainly because of confusing laws and state interference. The existing laws discourage foreign investment by allowing non-Iranians only 49 per cent of the shares in any venture and no right to own property. Strict labour laws are another deterrent to investment.

In the strategic industry of oil and gas exploration, foreign ownership is forbidden in the country's constitution, understandable given past experience. Instead, the government offers foreign firms the 'buy back' scheme under which these firms will finance specific projects. Repayment, including an agreed rate of return on investment, will take place over a specified period from a field's output. In spite of limitations of such a scheme the opportunities to secure a long-term position in the industry of one of the world's main oil and gas producers have enticed many oil exploration and development companies from western Europe, Russia and Australia to engage in negotiations for investment (*Financial Times*, 1 July 1998).

Like India and many other developing countries, Iran's protectionist policy is in part a reaction to political events. Iran has never lost its independence throughout its history, as did India for instance, but foreign powers such as the United States and Great Britain influenced the country's foreign and domestic policies, especially for the best part of the twentieth century. The Shah's father, the founder of the Pahlavi dynasty, came to power with the help of the British. Later, during the Second World War and because of his support for Hitler, the Allies, led by the United States and Britain, forced him to abdicate in favour of his son, who ruled the country under their patronage. A *coup d'état* in 1953, which entrenched his position of power in the country further, was staged by the Americans. This and similar historical episodes have created a need and desire in people for real political independence and economic self-reliance.

As a consequence of protectionist economic policies, however, business organisations are largely protected from both foreign competition and the rigour of a domestic market-based economy. In addition, Iran's economy is in the so-called 'demanding market' state, where demand outstrips supply. These two factors have in turn led to the almost total absence of a need for organisations to have vigorous market research, marketing, research and development and consumer relations and similar functions. There is little or no incentive for managers to emphasise product improvement and innovation. Iranian companies are, as a result, ill-prepared to face competition at home and abroad, and the country's bulk of export-related earning comes from crude oil, and not value-added manufactured goods.

A factor which distinguishes Iran from India is the former's vast oil resources. Iran is OPEC's second largest oil producer and accounts for roughly 5 per cent of the global oil output. The country holds 9 per cent of the world's oil reserves and 15 per cent of its natural gas reserves. Oil constitutes 85 per cent of export revenues as of 1996. This, following Porter's (1990) more general argument in this connection, has had significant bearing on the two nations' economic development. India may not be a star performer in the international market, but has achieved far more in terms of industrialisation and home-grown technology and manufactured goods than has Iran. It had its steel works and other heavy industries in place decades before Iran had hers. Almost everything that you come across in India is made in India, from hair pins to television sets, trains and planes. These may not be the best and the latest models, but they work and somehow fulfil people's ordinary day to day needs. A major reason for this 'self-sufficiency' is the absence of anything like the massive oil revenue that Iran has had for decades. Iran, in contrast and thanks to her oil reserves, has bought its way into modernity, industrialisation and consumer goods rather than making things indigenously.

Iran's and India's political economic policies could be further contrasted with the Southeast Asian tigers: Hong Kong, Taiwan, Singapore and South Korea, which have none of the rich natural resources of the first two countries and have only their human resources to fall back on. Interestingly enough they too were either largely colonies or under foreign powers' influence, or in the case of Taiwan excluded from many regional and global institutions, well into the twentieth century.

The region has long been an intellectual battleground for economists. Some saw these countries' rapid growth as proof of the virtues of market-friendly policies – low taxation, flexible labour markets and open trade. Others argued that South Korea's industrial policy was evidence of the possible gains from selective government intervention. The truth is that the economic policies of these countries vary hugely from relatively liberal Hong Kong to heavy-handed South Korea. However, they shared an openness to trade and higher savings than in other emerging economies.

There were indeed several factors which turned these countries into internationally competitive players in many manufacturing and service areas and which contributed to their spectacular economic take-off:

- First, they achieved their growth through export. Taiwan and South Korea, for instance, have few natural resources, little arable land, and the highest population densities of any country save Bangladesh and the city-states of Hong Kong and Singapore. The one policy that both have pursued is to be export-oriented. This simply means that they did not handicap their exports in world markets. Almost all developing countries do this, by bans, quotas or tariffs on imported goods. One of the disadvantages of trade restriction is that it both makes the home market more attractive to a might-be exporter, and also raises the cost of their imported input, so hampering them if they try to sell abroad. In partnership with the Japanese, South Korean and Taiwanese firms have penetrated new markets.
- Second, except South Korea to some extent, they actively encouraged foreign direct investment in their economies. Singapore's offer of generous tax breaks to foreign investors in the 1960s lured major oil refineries. These have made the country the world's third largest refining centre, after Houston and Rotterdam, even though the island republic produces no petroleum of its own and consumes only a small percentage of its refinery output.
- Third, as late developers, these nations utilised modern techniques and high technology in their efforts to pursue their policies and to achieve their economic objectives. Singapore is typical of the tigers. Lacking in major natural resources, Singapore must trade to survive. The information technology industry makes a crucial contribution to those export efforts and, in the process, it has modernised the entire business infrastructure. Indeed, Singapore owes its strategic position in the international trading network to its electronic links to global markets. To capitalise on the full potential of information

technology, Singapore formed a National Computer Board in 1981. Its objective was to establish Singapore as an international computer software services centre. Singapore has also poured millions of dollars into its utilities and infrastructure (for example, modern highways and an excellent underground system) and has underwritten R&D and office/science parks.

- Fourth, political stability in these countries in the past three decades or so has also played a significant role in their economic success. Their governments have pushed through development policies single-mindedly and with resistance to special-interest groups. Land reforms, for instance, were carried out in Taiwan by a dictator (Chiang kai Shek), and in South Korea by a government carried along by a wave of public anger at collaborators with the Japanese colonisers.

These countries, even though they have the appearance of a democracy and now respect civil liberties, have pursued an authoritarian regime throughout the period of their industrialisation and economic take-off. It was only in 1987 that the South Korean street riots drove the military out of office. Taiwan's gradual political reform started in the early 1980s and culminated in the end of martial law and a much freer electoral system only as recently as 1988. Singapore is still a virtual 'benign autocracy'. It is interesting to note that political reforms in these countries began only after they had achieved a high level of prosperity and growth. The handover to China of Hong Kong, never truly a democracy, took place without any political or economic instability and upheaval.

In short, the Southeast Asian tigers could be credited for getting right such fundamentals as macroeconomic stability, openness, allocation of resources, property and economic rights, physical capital, human capital and technology (Rowen, 1998; World Bank, 1993).

In China, the government does not appear to have plans to abandon the 'socialist-market economy' that was confirmed at the Communist Party's five-yearly congress in autumn 1997. This sanctioned a state-led form of development to take China through the post-Deng Xiaoping era. China's leaders talk enthusiastically of all the trappings of capitalism: foreign investment, 'modern-management systems', western 'shareholding structures', applied technology and so forth. But the state intends emphatically to remain master – appointing chiefs, urging strong companies to take over more decrepit ones, directing science, arranging credit and giving tax breaks. Under this ideology, outright privatisation is inconceivable for large companies, and bankruptcy out of the question.

The government aims to regroup large firms into a collection of conglomerates, modelled after the South Korean *chaebol*. But many small
state-owned firms have been, and are, targeted to be privatised. Development Chinese-style, a mixture of statism and lawless grabs for wealth,
has generated a dangerously skewed allocation of resources. Other
problems, such as misallocation of workers, financial mismanagement,
endemic corruption, a growing black economy and a high rate of unemployment, have had a negative effect on foreign investment, which fell
sharply in the early 1998 (*The Economist*, 14 February 1998).

Sometimes inaction or the absence of timely actions on the part of
the state could set a country back, in terms of competitiveness. The
United Kingdom's situation in the aftermath of the Second World War
is a case in point (Young, 1998). The country had won the war and was
still basking in the glory of this victory. However, the government,
which was among other things in charge of the economic well-being of
the country, seemed to have lost sight of the enormous efforts required
not only to make up for the economic costs of the war but also to catch
up with the defeated countries on the continent who were in full drive
to shortly become economic giants and new economic competitors to
the UK in the marketplace.

As Young points out, the prevailing view in the country at the time
took for granted Britain's capacity for independent decision-making in
any area her leaders chose. This rested on imperial sentiment and
national pride and the other outgrowths of the victory that saved Europe. But it also made assumptions about Britain's enduring economic
strength that did not entirely stand up to examination. The struggle
against Germany had been immensely costly. During the war, a quarter
of the national wealth, £7000 million, was lost: twice as much as in the
First World War and more, proportionately, than in any other combat-
ant country. The exports of this trading nation had not just declined but
plummeted: in 1944 they were only 31 per cent of their level in 1938.
The gold and dollar reserves were seriously run down, and in November 1945 it was necessary, with great difficulty, to arrange an American
loan of £3.75 billion.

In addition, although the speed of the postwar economic recovery
was impressive, especially on the exports side, it was less impressive
than that of other countries. In fact the nation's competitive decline
that was to continue for the next half-century started then. Growth
among the defeated or ravaged powers was consistently faster than it
was in Britain, and an assortment of reasons contributed to this. With
no unemployment and hardly any immigration, Britain had no surplus

labour to cope with expansion: the continentals had a surfeit. Britain had huge overseas obligations, not least the cost of policing the defeated countries: Germany and Italy had no such costs. Britain under a Labour government was preoccupied with wealth redistribution, and operated a top tax rate of over 90 per cent: on the continent there was far greater concern to create the incentives that would remake ruined economies.

Victory, in other words, produced decidedly less dynamic energy than did defeat. As a result, between 1947 and 1951, while British industrial production rose by 30 per cent, France and Italy achieved 50 per cent, and Germany 300 per cent. By the end of 1950, German production, after the devastation of the infrastructure, not to mention the controls imposed by the occupying powers, was back at prewar levels. It is true that in that year the British economy, measured by gross national product per head of the population, remained the second strongest in the world, with only the US ahead of it; but Germany and even France were closing steadily.

This was knowable at the time, according to Young; the trends and statistics were no secret. But it wasn't commonly apprehended, least of all in the quarters where it might have been most expected that the details would be closely studied, and the lessons honestly drawn. In government circles where victory in the war had done more to fortify the conceptions of the past than provoke new ones for the future, the evidence was received, as it were, blindfold (Young, 1998, pp. 22–4).

Before leaving this section, it might be useful to illustrate major characteristics of the economic policies of a few successful nations to provide a rough comparison with those discussed above. Table 2.1 provides this illustration.

MEMBERSHIP OF REGIONAL AGREEMENTS AND NATIONAL COMPETITIVENESS

Membership of economic and trade institutions, resulting in part from a government's favourable attitudes and policies to such memberships, can play a significant role in the respective countries' economic competitiveness. It gives the member states an additional tool with which they can provide a strong launching pad for their domestic firms and an attractive location for inward investment.

It is of course not easy to gauge reasonably accurately the impact of membership of regional agreement on the economic performance of member states, least of all because it is not possible to asses with any

Table 2.1 Economic policies of a selected group of nations

Country	Strong points	Weak points
• The US	Flexible labour and product markets, low taxes; fierce competition and shareholder capitalism, which puts pressure on managers to maximise profits	Wide income inequalities; low welfare benefits; poor quality of 'public goods', such as primary and secondary education; low investment and very low savings rates
• Japan	Lifetime employment encourage loyalty and high skill levels; public services, especially education, of high quality; close relations between banks and other firms; corporate cross-shareholdings shelter managers from impatient shareholders, allowing them to take a long-term view of investment	Some of these 'virtues' are now seen as vices: firms sheltered from the full force of the market feel little pressure to use capital efficiently
• Germany	Excellent education and training; a generous welfare state and narrow wage dispersion breed social harmony; close relations between firms and banks assist high investment	Overly powerful trade unions, high taxes, overgenerous jobless benefits and widespread labour and product market restrictions have led to persistently high unemployment
• Sweden	Relatively open markets combined with a comprehensive welfare state, narrow wage dispersion and employment schemes that push the jobless back into work	Rising inflation and recession increase the budget deficit, and as unemployment rises, costly job schemes are no longer affordable; high personal taxes blunt incentives to work
• New Zealand	Radical reforms in the 1980s; free-market; lowest tax rates; low trade barriers; widespread privatisation	Reforms resulted in a big increase in inequality

Source: *The Economist*, 10 April 1999, p. 90.

certainty a country's membership experience against a hypothetical no-membership alternative. How does, for instance, one assess what inward investors would have done if a country was not a member of a regional agreement? Inward investment is of course also affected by factors other than such memberships, such as the real exchange rate, tax rates, government incentives and labour market conditions. However, it is still possible to discuss the issue on principle, or even to some extent on the grounds of actual facts, as Münchau (1998) has done, for instance, for the UK. Münchau argues that the significant increase in the UK's exports to the other EU member states and the magnitude of the shift in her trading patterns with these nations since she joined the EU in the 1970s are of such a degree that it is difficult to find a reason other than EU membership.

The circumstances under which these political economic groupings are shaped, their primary objectives, and their evolution over time contribute to the extent of their success and its consequences for the economic competitive advantages of their member states. The European Union, came to being after the self-inflicted wounds the European nations suffered in the first half of the twentieth century. Germany and France in particular, which were and still are the main motors of the Union, wanted to lock themselves in a partnership which would prevent such wounds occurring in the future. The *raison d'être* of the Union was therefore primarily political, achieved through secondary economic objectives such as creaing employment after the war. Other nations, apart from notably Britain, shared largely similar political economic vision and determination and have been pressing ahead with the task of achieving their aims.

Also, notwithstanding a certain degree of cultural differences between the member states, there has been a great deal of similarities among them: the dominant religion (Christianity: same God, similar heritage, saints, institutions and rituals), broad philosophical views and thoughts, broad political and economic ideologies and beliefs, standard of living and economic prosperity, education and other socioeconomic institutions and their broad policies, high literacy rates and skill levels, broad citizen's rights and expectations, and so forth. These similarities have helped evolve and implement the political determination of the EU's founding fathers and their descendants. The same cannot be said about the disparate nations of Asia and Africa, for instance.

In Asia, there are many religions which dominate any single nation with sometimes fundamentally different views of life and how it should be organised: Hinduism, Buddhism, Islam, Judaism, Shinto, Confucianism:

their gods, their prophets, wise men and saints are different, their rituals and precepts are different, even their new years, religious fêtes and
sacred dates are different.

Other socio-cultural and political economic institutions, philosophies and priorities are also different. The nations range from those who
genuinely subscribe to and practise democratic values and institutions,
to those with authoritarian regimes and blatant abuse of human rights.
Economically, there is also a range from highly protectionist and closed-
door systems to the nearest that one can get to the pure *laissez-faire* capitalism. Levels of education and skills and literacy rates, standard of
living and the degree of industrialisation and economic advancement also
vary from the most advanced to those which seem to belong to bygone
centuries. Also, nothing like the horrors of the two world wars which
tore Europe apart has ever happened in Asia, certainly not in the twentieth century, barring the Hindu–Muslim bloody separation in the wake
of the British empire's departure from the Indian sub-continent. Other
conflicts such as the eight-year war between Iran and Iraq in the 1980s,
and border skirmishes between China and India, and those which dominated some of the south and central Asian nations, such as Vietnam
and Korean Wars, have not been of such a magnitude and nature to
force the nations involved to sit around a table and find a blueprint for
political economic integration to ensure a peaceful coexistence.

In Africa, these sorts of differences among nations have in addition
been overlaid by a particularly devastating colonial past, and a debilitating political and economic mismanagement in present times. It is beyond the scope of this chapter to discuss the complicated history of the
continent; suffice it to say that the outcome is a group of the most economically and politically disadvantaged nations which will take generations to build the kind of trust and unity of purpose needed to create
success stories such as the European Union.

The impact of membership in regional agreements and institutions
depends, moreover, on the nature of the pact. The European Union,
which is unique in terms of the depth and breadth of its integration,
offers many opportunities to both domestic firms and foreign inward
investors: a large unrestricted market, free movement of labour, capital, goods and services, freedom to merge and engage in joint ventures
and other strategic alliances, increasing deregulation across the board
in all member states, harmonisation of many of the rules and regulations which remain in place.

One of the major criticisms of the European single market in the past
has been the fact that with 15 different national currencies the exchange

of goods and services between member states would still be counted as imports and exports. The single market did not as a result have the benefits of the single-currency markets of Japan and the United States with which the EU was to compete on similar grounds. However, with the advent of the single European currency, the euro, operational in 11 of the EU nations from 1 January 1999, it was hoped that this problem would be removed. Moreover, it may be only a matter of time before other member states feel able on both political and economic grounds to adopt the euro as their national single currency.

It is true that the development of the EU since 1957 has been uneven and erratic. Nationalism, economic recession and enlargement of the Union have all served to delay and divert the process of European integration. Yet significant changes have occurred which have helped consolidate and strengthen the legal basis, institutional framework and policy-competence of the European Union. The attractiveness of such a large market (over 380 million people) with its vast potentials has drawn many multinationals, notably from North America, Southeast Asia and some non-EU-member nations of Europe.

As Clegg (1996) argues, countries outside the European Union, even the countries of the EFTA (European Free Trade Area), have an incentive to service the EU market from within. For instance, although tariff barriers might not form an obstacle, strategic considerations argue for production within the integrating market – to gain experience and improve competitiveness within the largest market in Europe, among others. These considerations, Clegg goes on to say, impart locational advantages to the countries within the integrating areas. NAFTA, the North American Free Trade Area, is largely concerned with breaking down barriers to trade between member states, namely the USA, Canada and Mexico. The latter, a developing nation making huge strides on her way to the 'rich man's club', seems to have gained enormously from membership of this free trade area, especially in the form of increased inward investment (see for instance Rugman and Gestrin, 1993).

Regional agreements in other parts of the world have not achieved the kind of status and significance as the EU and NAFTA have done for their respective member states, not to mention those which were stillborn. ASEAN (Association of Southeast Asian Nations) is a good example here. Formed in Bangkok in 1967, ASEAN's principal aims are to achieve peace and greater stability in the region, to advance the security of the member states (ASEAN was created at the height of the Vietnam war), and to assist the economic development of its members and encourage economic cooperation between them. However, the preferential trading arrangements between ASEAN's members, although growing, account for only a very small percentage of members' trade.

In the financial crisis which engulfed the region for much of 1997 and 1998, ASEAN which was above all designed to promote regional stability and economic health has not had much to contribute. It favours carrots over sticks, consensus over breakthrough, camaraderie over formality, and process over substance. Above all, ASEAN, unlike the EU, resists interference in the internal affairs of its members. Although this served the region well in the years after its founding in 1967, enabling old sores to be salved and mutual confidence to be built, it has rendered the organisation incapable of providing a concerted response to the financial disaster (*The Economist*,18 February 1998).

One of the ironies is that the economic integration to which ASEAN has always aspired has arrived in the saddest of circumstances. The group has made some progress in economic cooperation: intra-regional trade had been growing fast, lessening the reliance on America for exports, and a regional free-trade area is in the works; and there is some coordination between central banks. But the speed with which the markets turned on the region as a whole exaggerated its member countries' similarities, and the unity between them.

This contrasts sharply with the ways in which EU member states conduct their economic and political affairs – confronting difficult issues, albeit diplomatically pushing some temporarily under the carpet, but all the time moving forward with eliminating and resolving their differences and enhancing their integration.

Other attempts at creating an EU- or even a NAFTA-type institution in Asia have not yet been successful. A few years ago the Muslim countries of the continent, including those among the former Soviet republics, had the intention of creating an economic common market, but they could not agree whether or not to include the word Islamic in the title of the institution. The attempt came to nothing in the end. Further, as discussed earlier, there is a great deal of difference in the amount of political power and the level of economic and industrial advancement of many of the nations of the region, which is not conducive to an institution which has to be based on more or less equality of status for it to work, as is the case in many aspects between EU members. It is hard to imagine, for instance, nations such as China, India, Vietnam, Pakistan, Bangladesh, Iraq, Iran and Saudi Arabia sitting around the same table treating one another as equal partners or discussing economic issues of mutual interest.

One of the latest attempts at creating a trade agreement, this time covering certain countries in Asia and Africa, has been made by the Arabs. The Arabs, as a group of nations with much common cultural and religious heritage, have been trying to create a free trade area for years, and eventually at the beginning of 1998 an Arab Free-Trade Area (AFTA) was launched. But it is not certain that AFTA, whose current and would-be members are spread across two continents, will be more successful than similar past attempts. Earlier attempts at regional integration were largely political, based on the myth of Arab unity. The new treaty, signed by 18 of the Arab League's 22 members and designed to eliminate all trade barriers by 2008, is more firmly grounded in economics. Basically, it is a reaction to the bilateral Euro–Med agreements signed by the European Union and a number of countries south of the Mediterranean.

So far, these Euro–Med deals have been signed by three Arab states (Tunisia, Morocco and Jordan) and by Israel (which has a customs union with the Palestinian Authority). Algeria, Egypt, Lebanon and Syria are at the negotiating stage. The deals envisage the abolition of tariffs on industrial goods phased over 12 years, with some lowering of agricultural and service barriers. Since this implies the closure of many highly protected industries in Arab countries, the EU will provide money to help the Arabs restructure their economies.

AFTA is intended to create a climate which would entice inward investment in export-oriented industries, making the Arab world a global production centre. This will then accelerate growth, producing income tax to compensate for the loss of import duties which result from the breakdown of tariff barriers. There are, however, doubts as to whether this will work (*The Economist*, 10 October 1998). Arab countries offer very small markets, and AFTA will not offer many opportunities to achieve economies of scale. Official intra-Arab trade in 1997 was $15.5 billion, less than one-tenth of the total trade of Arab countries. In addition, transport and communications within the region are poor, thanks in large measure to public-sector monopolies, and this hampers regional integration. The free-trade scheme is also replete with exceptions (especially for farm goods, which make up a fifth of intra-Arab trade). An Arab League survey shows that even among the 12 countries that lived up to their promise to immediately reduce customs duties by 10 per cent, exempted goods outnumber those included.

An important point to note in connection with unions and other regional cooperation groupings among Asian and African nations, and indeed many other less-developed countries, is that these groupings often have purposes other than those officially stated. In many cases they represent the expression of a need – the determination to work together, to repudiate manipulation and interference from outside. This need exists mainly because many of these countries are economically, politically and militarily very weak. Moreover, as Arnold (1989) argues, it is one thing to state an aim, such as greater unity or cooperation; but it is something quite different to achieve the objective. The slow progress and seemingly futile arguments about trivia which have characterised the history of the EU serve to remind us just how difficult almost any form of international cooperation is, especially where the main aim is to achieve closer integration of sovereign nations. Moreover, unions are often not expected to work in the precise sense of two or more countries merging their sovereignty. They are, rather, expressions of the desire to work together.

SUMMARY

This chapter has likened nations to launching pads for their international firms and argued that the fates of the two are really intertwined, certainly before domestic firms are sufficiently strong to thrive at home and abroad even when their home-country's economy is in crisis (for example some Southeast Asian nations in the late 1990s). Political economic policies of governments have been argued to be major contributory factors in the success or failure of such launch pads. A comparison was made between a number of successful and unsuccessful nations to identify their policy strengths and weaknesses which could be said to be responsible for their current standing in international markets.

Open door, export-oriented policies of many established and emerging economies have helped them a great deal in becoming successful launching pads. Their domestic firms have not only learned from foreign firms, but they have also, through the competitive climate of the home market, gained experience and become seasoned for future battles on the international scene. Without being starry-eyed about such open-door polices, it was argued that protectionist measures taken by certain nations have held them back. These measures appear to reflect more than just the idiosyncrasies of politicians and their political and personal interests; they are in part rooted in historical events, such as being dominated or colonised by the superpowers of the time.

It takes time for these nations to trust 'foreigners', but there are signs that the past is being cautiously put behind and some of these countries are reaching out to foreign investors to come and assist them in their economic regeneration. Membership of regional trade agreements is also argued to play an important part in enabling home-based companies to venture successfully abroad. The chapter has discussed some of the political and historical reasons behind the success and failure of some nations to form such groupings in Europe, the Americas, Asia and Africa.

3 Organisational Competencies as Launch Pads for Internationalisation

INTRODUCTION

As we have seen in the first two chapters, at the macro level there are various sociocultural, economic and political institutions which are responsible for the kind of policies and practices that a country develops and implements. These in turn make up the resource pool from which companies may draw, internalise and then utilise. In other words, it was argued, national competitiveness is a significant factor in a company's ability to internationalise and become a major global player. Even though some companies might develop such abilities in spite of their home countries, they might still be hindered by their home government's policies to put their abilities to international practical use. Reliance, India's largest private-sector firm, for example, has all the qualities of a world-class player and in a recent study of competitiveness has been ranked as the most competitive firm in India and among the top ten in Asia (*The Economist*, 25 July 1998, p. 84). But what has in fact prevented it from becoming a global player is certain government regulations regarding capital movement overseas (letter by Reliance's Chairman in Europe, *The Economist*, 15 August 1998, p. 8).

However, national competitiveness is not sufficient to make an international star out of every company. It is ultimately the internal qualities of the company, such as managerial competence, technological know-how, financial and human resources, which would give it the inner strength necessary to exploit the potentials provided for it by its home country to launch itself overseas into greener pastures. This ability to utilise what is available is an asset which constitutes a part of their advantage over their rivals. As Whittington (1990) points out, it is important to recognise the plural and potentially contradictory nature of social structures, and the capacity of actors to draw upon these structures selectively and creatively. It is therefore argued that political and sociocultural factors, as well as numerous others, have a crucial role to play here.

MANAGERIAL COMPETENCIES AND NATIONAL CHARACTERISTICS

To compete effectively in domestic and international markets companies develop a unique set of skills for market positioning, combinations of resources, technologies and personnel that provide competitive differentiation (Harvey and Buckley, 1997). The core competency of a company not only becomes the distinct corporate signature, but also provides it with its competitive advantage (Hamel and Prahalad, 1990; Hall, 1993). Various aspects of management, from setting and implementing strategies (to be discussed in Chapter 6) to managing human and financial resources, production, marketing and other internal matters, to company–environment relationships, are obviously affected by the firm's core competency. This is in turn affected to some extent by external forces and actors, which are anchored to their political and sociocultural roots. The following sections will consider major managerial aspects in their wider context.

OBJECTIVES AND OBJECTIVE-SETTING

Organisations' objectives and the ways in which managers go about achieving them are of course crucial to their performance. Across nations, organisations may vary on both broad objectives and the means of realising them, not only in strictly business terms, but also in terms of the influences of their societal contexts on such matters.

In the United States and the United Kingdom, where there is widespread public share ownership, companies aim at increasing the dividends to be given to their shareholders, whose loyalty can be bought by a higher offer from another company. In other words, companies compete not only for customers but also the suppliers of capital, in the form of investors. A wave of hostile takeovers which especially characterises the British economy is a manifestation of such an intensively competitive capital market. The situation has resulted in the so-called short-termism of which British and American companies are regularly accused.

In Germany and Japan, on the other hand, public share ownership is far less widespread, and companies raise their required capital largely through borrowing from banks and other financial institutions. In Japan, especially, the lending banks even form a part of the larger conglomerate of which the individual company is a member. Cross-ownership and cross-board membership between banks and companies have traditionally accompanied such financial arrangements. As a result, these companies can afford to look into the future and adopt long-term objectives such as growth and market share, which do not yield significant financial rewards in the short and even medium terms.

The above-mentioned groups of companies, with different time perspectives and broad objectives, apart from making money in the long run have another feature in common: they are, other things being equal, outward looking, that is they can potentially include internationalisation as an option to achieve their goals and objectives. And their home-country institutions enable them, if they so wish, to set objectives with far away lands in mind. But in some other countries, especially in the developing world, this option might in practice be excluded from their companies' agendas.

Objective-setting in most developing nations has a dimension which is perhaps specific to their state of economy. Here, thanks to government intervention in business, companies might be required to achieve the government's social welfare goals through their normal commercial activities. India, for instance, like many other fellow third-world countries, lacks an extensive and well-developed national welfare state. People depend largely on their families and other relatives for help when they get old, or are sick or are without a job. Social issues such as poverty, unemployment and even ethnic problems are tackled through economic plans via business organisations.

Generally, labour-intensive technologies are encouraged in order to increase the level of employment. Quotas are set for companies to recruit workers from among lower castes and migrants from rural areas. Business firms, whatever their size, are encouraged to place themselves in 'backward areas'. They are told what to produce (for example, textile mills are required to supply a quota of cheap cloth for the poor) and, in many cases, how much to charge. There are also regulations and measures which make it almost impossible for managers to sack their manual workers or deduct from their wages even if they do not carry out their tasks properly. Partly to avoid making employees redundant and causing their families to suffer, the protection of inefficient firms has developed to such an extent that failed (the so-called 'sick') firms cannot close down under existing laws. Most sick firms are kept alive with subsidies, tax relief and credit extended by state-owned banks. Despite such measures and also regulated freight prices, costs tend to be higher in the backward areas. In other words, for many firms objectives are primarily set on social and not commercial and economic grounds. Such policies not only hinder further investment, growth and long-term planning, but also tend to make the firms involved inward-looking, all of which factors are detrimental to potential internationalisation prospects.

In many developing nations, companies' overall objectives can sometimes shape managerial roles as well. For instance, whereas in western countries managers' roles are largely confined within the 'four walls' of their companies, as it were; in developing countries their counterparts' domain stretches beyond their own organisation into the community. Social responsibility and participation in community affairs are not of course a monopoly of organisations in developing nations (see for instance Buchholz 1991; Smith *et al.*, 1996), but the scope and emphasis are much wider and deeper compared with more advanced nations (Muna, 1980; Tayeb, 1988; Das, 1991; Chow, 1992). In a country such as Iran or India it is a manager's social duty, for instance, to help bring electricity to his small town or improve the irrigation system in the neighbouring village. In a study conducted by Latifi (1997) in Iran, some of the managers interviewed said they would make their time and organisations available for high school and university students who wished to conduct research projects or acquire work experience as part of their courses. They saw this as fulfilling a part of their responsibility to the society and to the next generation of managers.

ACCESS TO TECHNOLOGY AND PRODUCTION FACILITIES

Factors which contribute to competitiveness of companies keep shifting all the time depending on general circumstances and changes in market conditions. There was a time that access to cheap natural resources or other factors of production would give a company, or a nation for that matter, an advantage over its competitors. Then came a time when the ability to manage and utilise such factors properly would differentiate between the competing actors. In our time, added to all this, is the knowledge and information factor as crystallised in the skills to produce and use electronics technology and to processes information, for example. Companies which have access to these new factors are more likely to succeed in the international marketplace compared to those which do not.

Also, real economic progress is the ability of the economy to produce those goods and services needed and wanted by society or, at least, to produce a large number of these and be able to export some of its excess production for the purchase of varieties not produced internally.

Technology plays an important role here. In a pertinent analysis Singer and Ansari (1982) make this point eloquently:

> When a rich country of today started its process of development it was an exporter of an agriculture-based product which had been processed, if at all, by simple and crude techniques; e.g. Britain exported textiles, Sweden exported timber and Canada exported wheat. As the process of development continued, export lines, like product lines, were shifted; e.g. Britain changed from exporting wool and cloth to exporting transport equipment, mechanical goods, electrical supplies, etc. In other words, the change of the technology of production manifested itself in the foreign trade structure of the countries concerned. (pp. 32–3)

By contrast, what seems to be happening in countries such as Iran and other oil-exporting nations of the Middle East, is not the indigenous development of appropriate technology but the purchase and transfer of technology from abroad. In this connection Sayigh (1982) argues that this transfer has come to be understood as the purchase of modern capital goods and the 'purchase' of the services of foreign technicians and experts. Nothing could be further from a genuine transfer of technology than such a course. What looks like a longer course of action, namely, the development of science, research, experimentation and technical training, is in effect the *true* short cut to technological capability.

Salvation here lies not in mere industrialisation as such, but rather in the development of indigenous scientific and technological capacities within these countries and in a reorientation of the present system of research and development which by and large ignores their needs (Singer and Ansari, 1982). Many developing countries are at a disadvantage compared to more economically advanced nations in this regard, in that they have poorly developed industrial and academic infrastructures and are far from the centres of science and innovation (Rowen, 1998).

Technology is of course crucial because of the role it plays in productivity. To nations which aspire to compete in the international market, what matters most is relative productivity. If a country's productivity grows more slowly than its rivals its competitive advantage will be lost. Moreover, changes in relative productivity growth affect a country's well-being. An economy that lags behind in productivity will also lag in incomes, that is, it will become (in relative terms) a low-wage economy. This will shift the pattern of comparative advantage in ways that feel painful; it will draw new investment from capital-intensive industries to labour-intensive ones. Britain, which until recently experienced a steady decline in productivity is an example from among industrialised nations. The country now attracts foreign investment more in its low-wage low-technology labour-intensive industries than it does in others (Tayeb, 1993). India can be cited among the developing nations with a low per capita productivity record.

Companies in many developing countries are still years, if not literally centuries, behind their more advanced counterparts with regard to modern technologies, especially of the information processing kind. The reasons for this state of affairs are legion but politics has a great deal to do with it. Information technology, for instance, could pose a serious threat and challenge to the absolute and semi-absolute powers that certain governments have. As a result, many companies are deprived of such facilities purely on political grounds. The use of telephone, fax machines, internet facilities and computers and consequently the flow of information are severely limited and controlled.

China is a good example here. Recently government has required the owners of cybercafés in Beijing to register their users and pass the names on to the Public Security Bureau. This move marks the Chinese government's determination to use the net's power as a communications tool while suppressing the ideas it may be used to communicate. Chinese net users are already required to connect to the Internet using only official gateways which block access to any web sites that might contain criticisms of the regime, views on Taiwan, or other non-conformist topics (*EasyLifeIP*, Issue 5, Spring 1999, p. 2).

Under such circumstances it is not possible to catch up with the latest developments and emulate the latest technologies. Product quality is an obvious victim of the situation. Companies' own strategies could also hinder or help their technological developments. Japanese companies, for instance, spend a great deal of money on their R&D work, compared to, say, their British counterparts. The Germans are more keen to get the quality of their products right rather than their marketing strategies, arguing that quality sells. The Americans go for both quality and marketing in their efforts to outperform competitors. Swedish companies add to their wealth of knowledge through acquisition of foreign companies with strong R&D units (Håkanson, 1995). In India, thanks mainly to the still largely protected domestic market and secure markets shares, R&D expenditure in many companies even in the electronics sector does not go beyond sending company representatives to a few international exhibitions from time to time (see also Tayeb, 1988).

Technology development is, as Bartholomew (1997) argues, embedded in a country's history, cultural values and attitudes. Societal institutions such as education, industry-university relationships, industrial structure and government policies, could all create socially embedded capabilities which the firms can in turn exploit. This does not of course mean that all firms operating in a given society can use these capabilities equally well. But the strongest and the more competent ones can take from what is on offer and make themselves competitive in the international market (Tayeb, 1995).

Attitudes to technology could also have something to do with national culture. Americans, for instance, are future-oriented and strongly inclined to believe that present ways of doing things are inevitably to be replaced by even better ways. By contrast, the British are known for their love of the past, and for them the view of history is essentially to accept the present as a culmination of past developments and, therefore, as representing the highest achievement attainable (Dubin, 1970). The Americans' future-oriented attitude, one could argue, is immensely helpful as a foundation for technological innovation and the use of new technologies, while the British past-orientation might be unhelpful in this regard, to say the least. This does not, of course, mean that the British are less innovative in scientific and technological fields, but it is true that in the implementation of innovative ideas and inventions they lag behind their counterparts in countries such as Germany, the USA and Japan. Many British inventions and product prototypes have in the past been taken up and converted to commercial products by foreign companies. The compact disc (CD) and computer are examples of British inventions which were developed by Japanese and American companies, respectively, and turned into what they are now.

BUILDING A CUSTOMER BASE

One of the factors which helps launch a company to a favourable position in the international market is a large domestic customer base, and one way of achieving this is through getting the products known by potential customers. Advertising and marketing strategies and techniques are an obvious vehicle here.

There are various ways and means that companies situated around the world can exploit in order to create, maintain and increase their customer base. For instance, as mentioned earlier, American companies have always used various marketing strategies, whereas German companies, in general, have traditionally been reluctant to place a great emphasis on or to invest in marketing and advertising functions, instead they consider the quality of their products a major selling point. Many British companies also held attitudes similar to the Germans until the recent past (see for instance, Jamieson, 1980; Locke, 1985; Handy, 1988; Reid, 1989; Gordon, 1990). Notwithstanding these differences in approach and preference, what all these companies and their counterparts in the liberal industrialised world have in common is the availability and freedom to use various techniques and media to get their products known to their potential customers. For them the potential is virtually limitless, provided that their internal resources allow them to use it. All sorts of mass communication media, from the humble billboard to written press, radio, television and the Internet can be employed to circulate the information the companies may wish to reach their customers. Those who can afford it either recruit professionals and specialists for in-house production, or contract out their marketing functions, the deciding factors in any case being mainly their policies and strategies.

Customer-reach, however, is far more limited for companies in some less-advanced nations, not only for technological and financial reasons but also for sociocultural ones. Religion, social taboos and customs, for instance, set limits to the way in which a commercial advertisement is worded or depicted. A low literacy rate, limited access to radio, television and electronic or written press may further hamper a company's ability to use market research or other sophisticated marketing and advertising techniques. In addition, in some countries governments restrict the use of such media and the manner of their use by commercial enterprises. As a result they are deprived of a crucial avenue to increase their customer base to achieve economies of scale and build enough strength and experience to feel able to venture into the outside world.

The quality of the customer base, in terms of sophistication, expectations and income, or what Porter (1990) refers to as demand conditions, is of course a significant factor. Here again there is a vast gap between the rich industrialised nations and what they can offer their domestic firms, and their poorer less economically advanced counterparts. For a vast majority of the population in many of the latter nations quality is a luxury and the bare essentials can only be afforded: one eats food to survive, it does not matter if it is not made with free-range chicken and organically-grown vegetables; one needs to get to one's place of work every morning to earn a decent living, it does not matter if it is not in the latest model of a well-equipped hatchback car, and so forth.

As a result, many domestic companies are not under significant pressure, if at all, to make the products which are beyond the reach of the majority of their potential customers. And, more importantly, there is no incentive to improve quality because of the lack of serious competition, which is usually the case in the protected markets of many developing nations. Local producers can usually sell whatever they produce even if they leave much to be desired. This is not to say that quality products do not exist in such countries, they certainly do (even Egypt and Libya have their Bennetton franchised producers and retail outlets). But these products are usually targeted at a small, rich and sophisticated niche market which may or may not provide a strong enough base for the companies involved from which to launch into international markets.

THE MANAGEMENT OF HUMAN RESOURCES

Human resource management (HRM), by definition, considers employees as a resource and production function, alongside capital, land, raw materials and technology, in need of management, even though they cannot easily be moved around, shuffled, reduced, increased, transformed and discarded as can other factors. Employees are, in addition, some of the most crucial resources in the company on which its prosperity depends to a large extent. As Campbell (1988) points out, employee's higher productivity, leading to lower costs and greater motivation, and leading to better service, can both result in competitive advantage. Recognised as such, as some companies do, human resources have to be managed with tact and care, for the interests of everybody concerned. Companies which succeed in doing so thereby have a competitive advantage over their rivals.

The 'economic miracle' of the Asian tigers, which catapulted them over the last three decades or so from a state of underdevelopment to that of highly competitive players in the international market, has in the opinion of many observers and commentators been to a large extent due to their competitive advantage in human resources. They achieved this advantage at the micro level through training policies and management style, and at the macro level through national education policies and practices. Indeed, these nations have hardly any natural resources other than their people. Economic and trade policies, as we saw in the previous chapter, also helped things along.

HRM is influenced both by internal (company) and external (country) factors. Company objectives and national culture are examples of such factors used in the following comparison between Japan and the United States to illustrate this point. Both American and Japanese companies are essentially capitalist entities and ultimately pursue profit maximisation. They both have to tackle issues such as economic recession, labour costs, competition and the like. However, their approaches and ways of handling things may be different. A Japanese company might choose, in response to economic downturns, to reduce labour costs by cutting the managers' pay; its American counterpart might respond to similar conditions by laying off a great number of manual workers, some white-collar employees, and a paltry 1 per cent pay cut for the executives (*The Economist*, 24 November 1990). The roots of these different approaches can be traced to their respective socio-cultural backgrounds (Tung, 1984; Briggs, 1988; Tayeb, 1995; Tayeb, 1996a).

The Japanese employees' and employers' behaviours might have something to do with their collectivism, the inclusion of the workplace in their in-group, their sense of duty and indebtedness to one another as members of a group, and their attitude to face-saving. The Japanese suffered a humiliating loss of face in the Second World War. The determination to excel economically in the world has intensified the group cohesion among the members of society and the feeling of being part of a big family. Americans, on the other hand, are an individualistic nation where people mainly pursue their own interests and those of their immediate family – the in-group definitely does not include the workplace. The primary commitment and loyalty of individuals do not therefore lie with the company or any other larger grouping of which they may be a member.

These characteristics seem to have been reflected in the culture of business organisations as well. American and Japanese companies and employees differ fundamentally in the extent to which they are committed to one another. This in turn influences the management style and HRM policies in the two countries. The Japanese company considers its employees as an asset, rather than a liability; it invests in their development; it has a long-term view of their relationships; and hires the employees (especially the skilled core workforce) on a long-term basis. It trains them through rotation in various functional departments in order to enhance their flexibility. Employees, in return, display a high degree of commitment and loyalty to their work organisation. The American company, on the other hand, and its employees have a short-term perspective. The employees join their work organisation as a step in their career development ladder, and leave the company when better prospects beckon elsewhere. The company, on its part, hires and fires its employees at will, and recruits them in order to fill specified skill slots; flexibility is not a primary concern.

The above kind of attitude to employees is exemplified in the advice recently given to Germany by the American news magazine *Time*. The magazine identified high unemployment as one of the major problems of the German economy, and advised politicians to accelerate labour-market reform to allow easier hiring and firing of workers (*Time*, 14 September, 1995, p. 28).

The above comparison also serves to remind us that the combination of micro and macro factors which influence HRM are never the same across organisational and national borders. As a result, instead of the adoption of universal, so-called 'best practices' firms might strive to arrive at HRM styles which best suit their objectives and at the same time are practicable, given their sociocultural context. The socio-cultural context could, of course, have both helpful and harmful effects on HRM at national and company levels, and in turn on international competitiveness. But it also depends on how cultural characteristics are managed and incorporated into the organisational way of life by the management team. In other words, national context need not be a straitjacket.

Japanese, Indians, Iranian and the so-called Asian tigers are all known to be hard working, resourceful and collectivist, and committed to group interests, among other things. But what is interesting to note is that the Japanese and other Asian tigers appear to have been able to build on the cultural characteristics of their people and incorpor-ate them into their organisational culture: quality circles thrive on col-lectivism (Tayeb, 1990), *ringi* decision-making cushions employees against individual risk-taking (Hofstede, 1980), and close management–subordinate relationships provide an atmosphere of emotional support (Tung, 1984, 1988). In Japan this has further led to the workplace being a part of the employees' in-group (Tayeb, 1994). This situation is cer-tainly not the case in Iranian and Indian organisations (Tayeb, 1979, 1988, 1998). It is true that the high degree of employee commitment in Japan and other Southeast Asian countries, and the low commitment in India and Iran, also have other explanations beside culture (Briggs, 1988; Tayeb, 1988; Tayeb, 1990), but culture plays a significant part in these states.

India is rich in human as well as other natural resources. A review of the literature shows that Indians are resourceful and hard working, have a keen sense of responsibility, are thrifty and entrepreneurial, and are ambitious and materialistic. And as many of us who live in western societies observe in our day-to-day life, a vast majority of the Indian immigrants who have settled in these societies have done very well indeed in various walks of life, be it academia, business or professions, and prospered. As an Indian industrialist puts it, 'overseas Indians have successfully faced competition in their host countries. There is no reason why Indians can't do the same in their own country if they are given the same opportunities' (*Time*, 10 January 1994, p. 27).

A likely explanation for why Indian people do not succeed in their own home country as much as they do abroad is that some Indian leaders and managers have systematically mismanaged these valuable but at the same time low-cost human resources. The extent of employee productivity is one of the criteria by which one can judge a country's performance in the management of human resources. Various annual reports of the World Bank show the productivity of Indian employees has for a long time been far lower than their counterparts in Japan and other Southeast Asian countries. In addition, Indian organisations, especially in the public sector, which cover major heavy and strategic industries are bedevilled by corruption, a symptom of the lack of commitment to organisational goals and objectives.

In Iran, too, companies suffer from culturally-induced obstacles which are holding them back from competitiveness in domestic and international markets (Tayeb, 1999a). Iran's is a predominantly collectivist culture with a heavy infusion of Islamic values. Fear of God, piety and abstinence, decency, truthfulness, helping the poor and weak, respect for age and seniority, hospitality, loyalty, obedience of leaders and looking up to seniors for direction, family-orientation, uncertainty avoidance, and fatalism yet acceptance of responsibility for one's actions, are among the Islamic roots of the Iranian culture. The extent to which these ideals are translated into practice is, however, a different matter. They are by their nature open to interpretation, and the workplace is a notoriously fertile ground for such interpretations given its varied constituencies, interests and goals. Moreover, Islam is not the only source of Iranian national character.

Throughout its long history, the nation has experienced many unpleasant and hard times as well as happy episodes: authoritarian regimes, repression, wars, domination and invasion by foreign powers and loss of territory. Some of these events have created a deep scepticism and distrust in the national psyche and a need to take refuge in the security offered by religion and in the comfort of home and family, which alone alongside God can be trusted.

The implications of such a psyche for the management of organisations are obvious. From the employees' point of view, the workplace
does not belong to their in-group, as is the case for example in Japan.
Their commitment to the company is at best shaky and at worst open to
negotiation. As a consequence, corruption in many institutions and organisations, especially in the public sector, is endemic. Also, employees'
willingness to participate in the decision-making process and the running of the organisation, particularly at middle and lower levels, is
almost non-existent. From the management side, there is a deep mistrust
in subordinates. As a result, organisations tend to be centralised, with
power concentrated in the hands of a few and trusted senior managers.

In a study of 14 organisations in pre-revolutionary Iran, Tayeb (1979)
found some of the managers who had been educated in American and
European universities to be aware of the merits of decentralising
decision-making in their organisations as an appropriate response to
their changing environment, but they were reluctant to employ such an
approach in their own companies. They did not trust their subordinates' abilities and intentions to carry out their tasks properly. Indeed,
these managers argued that they would stand to benefit if they tight-
ened their control over their employees and made important decisions
themselves. Some had chosen to appoint their own close friends and
relatives to crucial posts, thereby to ensure the proper handling of the
organisation's tasks.

In post-revolutionary Iran, Bani-Asadi (1984), Mortazavi and Karimi
(1990) and Mortazavi and Saheli (1992) found that in the organisations
they studied managers in general tended to adopt a paternalist
approach, which has the benefit of centralisation but also has a kinder
and softer touch. It is also more in line with Islamic teachings, which
have been emphasised since the 1979 revolution. These teachings
advocate equality before God; individual responsibility within a framework of cooperation with others; a view that people in positions of
power should treat subordinates kindly, as if their subordinates are
their brothers or sisters; encouragement of consultation at all levels of
decision-making, from family to the wider community and the country
as a whole (Latifi, 1997).

In order to be successful at work and create a friendly atmosphere Iranian managers attempt to build a close and heartfelt relationship with
their subordinates. This point is supported by Latifi's (1997) research.
She closely observed a small sample of Iranian managers at work over a
period of time and found that Iranian employees viewed their managers as sympathetic brothers and sisters or compassionate fathers and

mothers. In addition, this family-like relationship appears to have been extended to include 'social' and 'teacher' roles for the managers. They were frequently involved in their subordinates' private lives and family matters.

In the euphoria which followed the 1979 revolution, people took pride in their collective action which led to the overthrow of the Shah's authoritarian regime. The country became for a while a big united family. Some of this euphoria and the shared experience might also explain the paternalistic and soft touch of some organisations. However, notwithstanding the positive influence of certain aspects of Islam on Iranian culture and its incorporation into some organisations, some deep-rooted cultural and non-cultural impediments and constraints to managerial professionalism and employment of innovative and modern management techniques still remain (Tayeb, 1998, see also Chapter 2). As a result, Iranian managers have limited strategic and organisational choices at their disposal. Using a musical metaphor, Tayeb (1979) argued that these managers have a low repertoire of modes of structure and management styles. Organisations that she studied tended to be highly centralised, formalised and standardised, irrespective of the diversity of their specific task environments and contextual factors, such as industry, product, technology, size, market share and ownership.

This low repertoire also limits the managers' ability to import and modify management practices such as participative decision-making, quality circles, total quality management, teamwork and the like (Tayeb, 1995). These practices presuppose, among other things, a willingness to participate in group decision-making and decision-implementing and a strong commitment to the workplace on the part of employees. They also assume a certain degree of confidence and trust in employees and a willingness to delegate authority to team members on the part of their managers. Iranian culture does not appear to be as fertile a ground for such management practices as was Japan's when Japanese managers successfully imported them from the United States a few decades ago. Consequently, Iranian companies are hampered in their efforts to respond to market conditions quickly and appropriately, to gain enough inner strength to take on their well-seasoned competitors abroad, and to become major players in the international market.

A similar combination of cultural and non-cultural factors have, in different ways and at a different level, pushed and pulled British companies, sometimes in opposite directions, with regard to their international business position. The characteristics that are most significantly present in British culture and which are more likely to have a bearing on the British business climate and approach to management are individualism, deference and acceptance of inequality, self-control and reserve, conservatism, xenophobia, honesty and trust, regard for liberty, class consciousness and the resulting 'them and us' attitudes among the workforce, and low respect for commerce and manufacturing compared to finance and stockmarket professions.

British managers, brought up in such a culture, tend to be very polite, tenacious, resourceful, reserved and self-disciplined (Terry, 1979); but at the same time they generally have ethnocentric attitudes towards their foreign counterparts. As mentioned earlier, British managers are said to have a short-term perspective in their business planning (at least relative to the Japanese); they spend too little on R&D and on employee training relative to their annual turnover; they have a conservative approach towards new technology; and they place more emphasis on the production rather than the marketing side of their business, compared to their major competitors such as American, Japanese and French managers.

There are also non-cultural as well as cultural explanations for some of these attitudes. Take the managers' short-term perspective, for example. The City is one of the major sources of capital for most British companies. Investors, both individuals and institutions, seek above all a quick return on their investment, which puts managers under immense pressure to go for the 'quick buck'. They do not have the luxury of the long-term financial support that their Japanese counterparts enjoy in their cosy relationships with banks and government. R&D is an obvious victim of this situation. Employee training (and the consequent improvement in productivity) is another. Product quality is the third. The list can go on

Two recent studies suggest that British productivity is way below that of other western countries such as the United States, France and Germany. McKinsey (1998), a consultancy firm, concludes in its report that the US labour productivity (measured by output per hour worked) is 37 per cent ahead of Britain's; and that of Germany and France is around 25 per cent ahead. Another study, by O'Mahony (1998) of the National Institute of Economic and Social Research, puts all three 20–30 per cent ahead of Britain.

British managers' reluctance to allocate a great deal of time and financial resources to employee training may also have a 'foot' in the country's national culture. British employees, like many other individualistic people, and unlike the Japanese 'company man', pursue occupational advancement through their career rather than, or as well as, their work organisation. Job-hopping and moving from company to company are the rules of the game, rather than life-time employment and cradle-to-grave commitment to one company. As a result, British managers see expenditure on training as a waste of their precious capital, and not as an investment in human resources. It is worth noting here that the Americans are probably more individualistic than the British, and US firms have a similar short-termist approach to return on investment, and raise capital in similar markets to their UK counterparts. But they spend much more on employee training.

McKinsey's report also diagnoses the shortage of skills, among others, as one of the main problems for British firms. Although Britain now produces plenty of graduates, it has a higher proportion of workers with poor skills or no qualifications than Germany. And American firms, faced like their British counterparts with a high proportion of unskilled workers, make a far better job of training them for specific jobs.

The relatively poor quality of some British products (Trought, 1989) is not unexpected given the economic context of the firms. Within the decade between the early 1980s to the early 1990s, recession hit British firms twice. Moreover, the government's open-door policies subjected these firms to fierce competition from Japanese, German and American rivals, among others. Many managers were forced to go for lower quality in order to keep their prices down. A speech by the chairman of a large jewellery retail-chain firm, in which he told his audience that his company sells rubbish to customers at cheap prices (BBC Radio 4 news and commentary programmes, 23 April 1991), illustrates how some companies were left with precious little alternative.

To an outside observer, such as the present author, it seems that history, ecology and a long-drawn out evolutionary process have created in Britain a culture and social climate which stand British managers and their companies in good stead in many respects, but handicap them in others (Tayeb, 1993). Their honesty, frankness, trust, self-control, self-discipline and politeness are their major cultural assets. The sometimes explicit xenophobic tendencies displayed by some British managers work against their business interests, especially when there are more receptive competitors across the Channel. A vast majority of British firms, thanks to the economic climate and the government's open-door policies, are willing and quite competent to deal with competitive markets. But at the same time they are hampered in their efforts by unhelpful and sometimes downright harmful aspects of their culture and their society. These include capital market short-termism, less-than favourable attitudes to business, traditionalism and a reluctance to embrace new technology whole-heartedly, antipathetic industrial relations, and ill-prepared school leavers and university graduates. To an outside observer, the situation resembles a perfectly decent vehicle whose driver has put his feet on the accelerator and brake pedals simultaneously! It is a tribute to the resourcefulness and resilience of British businessmen and women that their country occupies such a high rank in the league of industrialised nations.

ABILITY TO ADOPT FOREIGN PRACTICES

Many managers understandably attempt to learn from their more successful counterparts elsewhere. There seems to be, however, some sociocultural and political economic characteristics which are more conducive to the success of such cross-border learning processes than others.

The Japanese for instance were very successful in importing certain US-grown management techniques and ideas and adapting them to their own local specifications. It is, for instance, well-known that practices such as quality circles were introduced into Japan by Americans such as Deming and Jurdan who arguably helped bring about Japan's postwar production miracle. Finding that their ideas about total quality management evoked little interest in the United States, they discovered more fertile ground elsewhere (Hodgson, 1987). It is arguable that in Japan's case this fertile ground was her culture, which could accept and use these US-grown ideas. One of the prerequisites for the successful implementation of quality circles, for example, is a high degree of commitment by employees to their company and its goals – a characteristics that is attributed to most Japanese employees. But Iran's similar attempts to adopt American models in the 1950s and 1960s were a total disaster.

British companies, to give another example, have been able to import a number of foreign practices such as quality circles, team work, flexible working patterns, just-in-time and total quality management from Japan, and cell manufacturing from Scandinavia. In a series of case studies of British and foreign firms operating in Scotland (Tayeb, 1998; Tayeb, 1999b; Tayeb and Dott, 2000), the present author found that they had imported these practices and implemented them successfully after certain modifications to suit their own circumstances. In the case of three manufacturing firms, these foreign practices had in fact helped them fight back a threat of certain 'death' (Tayeb, 1999b). Training, management style and the senior managers' determination and the rank-and-file workforce's basic technical skills and willingness to learn new ways of doing things were major factors which enabled a successful process of importation and implementation of foreign practices.

Another factor, freedom of citizens to travel abroad, especially for professional and educational purposes, could help immensely the process of learning from others: a kind of freedom which is taken for granted in many democracies. *The Economist*'s (14 September 1996) introduction to one of its articles, commenting on the travelling habits of managers from such countries, demonstrates the 'matter of courseness' of such freedoms: Today's ambitious managers spend their holidays not on the beach, but on pilgrimages to the world's best-run companies. They visit Florida's Disney World, to study Uncle Walt's 'pixi dust' formula for managing people, or small American firms such as Springfield Re-Manufacturing and Johnsonville Sausage which have pioneered new fads, or visit Toyota City to learn about lean production.

Managers pay such visits abroad with the primary intention of improving their own companies' performance (Womack *et al.*, 1990; Osterman, 1994; Macduffie, 1995). But, for political and economic reasons, managers from many societies, like most of their compatriots, cannot or even are not allowed to avail themselves of similar opportunities. Moreover, for similar reasons these countries suffer from a debilitating brain drain which all but deprives their domestic firms of a skilled and conversant workforce and discourages inward foreign investment. Such brain drains and impediments to movement and learning do not exist among the liberal and economically advanced countries which dominate the international markets of our time.

One of the factors which, for instance, helped the industrialisation and economic take-off of Taiwan was the attractiveness of the country to expatriates. They flocked back home to participate in the building of its 'miracle' (Hsu, 1999). India, by contrast, has been unsuccessful in making the country equally attractive for its expatriates (*The Economist*, 25 July 1998).

The return of expatriates is not of course confined to people but can encompass capital as well. Chinese people living and working overseas have been very good at investing in their original homeland, China. This again contrasts sharply with the situation in India. Since 1991 the Indian government has been issuing five-year bonds, some in foreign currency for sale specifically to Indians living abroad, counting mainly on their patriotism. However, unlike China which because of its economic boom has attracted expatriates' inward investment, India's poor economic performance has not had the same effect on her expatriates. After seven years or so of economic reform in India, expatriates' investment in local markets and businesses remains very small. Portfolio investment and foreign direct investment by Indians abroad has tailed off sharply since 1996 (*The Economist*, 25 July 1998).

Foreign firms with local operational units could be a good medium and role model for local companies to learn new management techniques and practices, even though there may initially be scepticism and resistance, not to mention xenophobia, towards such foreign imports. The present author in a series of interviews in the mid-1980s found such sentiments, accompanied by disparaging remarks, among some British senior managers towards Japanese management styles in two-way and three-way joint ventures involving Japanese partners located in south-east and south-west Britain (Tayeb, 1994). However, now a decade or so later such practices are seen as a useful means to increase employee productivity and achieve efficiency in production processes (Tayeb, 1998, 1999b). This learning opportunity is missed, sometimes completely, in the business environment of local firms operating in protected and semi-protected economies. As a result, they are out of touch with the latest techniques which could help them improve their performance in general and the quality of their HRM in particular.

Another avenue to learning from others is for domestic firms to buy up or engage in joint ventures with firms in similar lines of business located abroad to learn their technological and managerial know-how. This avenue, again, is open only to the companies whose home-country government allows free flight of capital to destinations beyond their national borders. As we know this is not the case in many protectionist, closed-door, or even semi-open-door nations, where local companies' hands are tied behind their back by politics.

SUMMARY

Company-level resources and competencies have been argued in this chapter to be necessary for a firm to build up enough strength and experience to venture abroad. The goals that a company sets for itself, its HRM skills, access to appropriate technologies and the ability of its workforce to operate them, building and maintaining a large customer base, and the ability to learn and adopt foreign 'best practices' are among the internal capabilities that help form a successful company at home and abroad. It has been argued that these capabilities are to a large extent embedded in the company's home country. The absence or shortage of these sets severe limits to what a company can do in order to go out and succeed in international markets.

In certain countries, national culture, political and economic institutions and their policies and management, educational preferences and practices have all 'conspired' to make life difficult for managers with any ambition to go international. By contrast, in other countries, favourable conditions regarding some or all of these factors have increased the chances of domestic firms to build up their internal strengths and become successful internationally as well as domestically.

4 Motives and Limits to Internationalisation

INTRODUCTION

This chapter explores why certain firms would want to expand overseas in the first place and discusses different motivations that they might have for becoming multinational. Furthermore, we examine whether or not there are limits to internationalisation and globalisation.

The prime objectives of any business organisation are to make profits, grow and increase its market power. Companies engage in international business when the possibility of achieving these objectives are either diminishing at home and/or there are great opportunities abroad. The literature is awash with discussions on motives behind a company's decision to go beyond its home-country boundaries. There is also a lively debate going back over three decades among various scholars regarding the internationalisation process and entry-mode strategies (Vernon, 1966; Wells, 1968; Buckley and Casson, 1976; Bilkey, 1978; Johanson and Vahlne, 1977; Rugman, 1980; Cavausgil, 1980; Dunning, 1980; Reid, 1986; Root, 1987; Young, 1987; Buckley, 1988; Dunning, 1988; Toyne, 1989; McKiernan, 1992; Wheeler *et al.*, 1996). The intention in the present chapter is not to provide a critique of the models and theories offered so far, a task which has been excellently performed by Bell and Young (1998) and Melin (1997), among others, but rather to discuss some of the cultural and political factors which might influence firms' decisions to internationalise and set limits on how far they can implement such decisions.

WHY INTERNATIONALISE?

Broadly, internationalisation motives would fall into three categories: those related to the home country, the host country(ies) and the company's own core competencies. Apart from the importance of the home country in a company's internationalisation as a launching pad, discussed in Chapters 1 and 2, there are other so-called push factors in the home-base, some positive and others negative, which would encourage business organisations to go abroad. Among the positive factors, as we saw in earlier chapters, are a government's export-oriented economic and trade policies, the removal of foreign exchange control and reduction or removal of tariffs on imported capital goods and on the recruitment of foreign employees with the needed technical and managerial expertise, and so forth.

Among the negative push factors which would make investment in home markets less attractive than in the foreign ones, are market saturation or even a lack of market, fierce competition from domestic and foreign companies, a high cost of production (wages, raw material, capital, land) and a shortage of the required managerial and technical skills. There may also be restrictive regulations at home which some firms might prefer to avoid. Regulations concerning reserve requirements, deposit insurance or corporate taxes, for instance, have prompted many US banks to move all or parts of their operations abroad and to set up subsidiaries in countries with less stringent rules. Many of these factors have their roots in the government's overall political and economic ideologies and policies which, intentionally or unintentionally, result in domestic firms going abroad for better opportunities.

There are many pull factors in other countries in addition to those discussed in earlier chapters that may entice companies to invest abroad. Closeness to raw materials, the availability of resources and advanced technology, and the so-called 'follow your customer' principle can be powerful attractions to encourage firms to invest abroad. In some cases, notably in the case of many Japanese firms, suppliers of services and semi-finished components might follow their main commercial customer overseas, for instance a memory-chip producer might go where its bigger 'sister' computer firm goes.

Sometimes firms decide to get into a foreign market because their competitors are already there or are planning to do so, and they do not want to be left behind. The rush of many companies from the capitalist world to China and the ex-socialist countries in central and eastern Europe is, in part, an example of this. In addition, these countries have largely untapped markets, resulting mainly from unsatisfied customers' demands for quality products, and new opportunities such as poor and outdated infrastructure in need of fundamental upgrading. Companies may want to get a 'foot' in a market the entry to which might become harder later. The rush of investment in EU member countries by foreign firms, especially the Japanese and Americans, prior to the enactment of the Single Market in 1992 was motivated by the desire to become 'good Europeans'. The Single Market was seen then, and still is perceived by many, as 'Fortress Europe' erected to protect domestic companies against non-Europeans.

High unemployment rates and weak trade unions in the target areas could be a good reason for foreign direct investment. Many of the Japanese plants recently set up in the UK, for instance, were attracted to that country because anti-union laws since the early 1980s have rendered British unions virtually powerless. Japanese managers could therefore push through their single-union and no-strike deals with the workers' representatives (Tayeb, 1994). The reduction of the power of trade unions was essentially motivated by political considerations (Hatton, 1995; Marr, 1995), but it had economic spin-offs, such as labour market deregulation, which contributed to the attractiveness of the country from the foreign investor's perspective.

The type of workforce that companies need, for example unskilled workers for humdrum jobs, highly skilled ones for technically advanced tasks, and hard working and committed employees, can also be a factor in deciding to go abroad. A recent case study conducted by the present author (unpublished work-in-progress manuscript) in an American company located in the central belt of Scotland provides an interesting example. The Scottish subsidiary until 1997 performed all the usual major functions, from manufacturing to marketing and sales, employing altogether 250 people. The parent company in conjunction with the Scottish plant's American managing director, decided two years ago to relocate the manufacturing part of their operation to Hungary. The relocation was completed in June 1999, laying off 150 Scottish employees in the process. The two reasons for the relocation were the distance from the company's main European market and their Scottish workforce's resistance to the parent company's preference for the American management style, a resistance that the company does not face in Hungary.

In Budapest, the HQ is importing wholesale its American style of management, from manufacturing techniques to health and safety procedures to HRM to their newly acquired subsidiary. The expatriates find the Hungarians very receptive to these imported practices and styles and have accepted all the restructuring and reorganisation which the new American owners proposed and implemented even if at times these reduced the power and control of the local managers. For instance the financial powers of the former MD of the Hungarian company has been reduced considerably, so have his scope of operation and authority. He is now in charge of only a segment rather than the whole of the operation. Moreover, he reports to the American MD who is currently running the Scottish as well as the Hungarian operations, rather than directly to the HQ.

Investing in two or more countries can help reduce risks – the principle of 'not putting all one's eggs in one basket'. By doing so, companies can offset economic troughs in some countries against the peaks in others, and benefit overall. Sometimes it is cheaper to manufacture goods in a foreign country than to export them to it. Major deciding factors, of course, would be the cost of labour (wages), raw materials, capital (interest rates) and transport.

Some governments offer various incentives such as tax concessions and grants, or impose import tariffs and quotas in order to persuade foreign direct investors to set up plants in their countries. Their main aims are usually to bring in capital, know-how and technology, to create jobs for their citizens locally, and to diversify their industrial base. Policies of this kind are not of course confined to developing countries, as some might think. The British government, for example, has enticed many multinational companies, especially from the EU states, Japan and other Southeast Asian nations, to the less economically-prosperous regions of the country by offering them grants and other concessions. The same policy is also employed from time to time to encourage some of the existing foreign companies, which threaten to close down their British subsidiaries for various productivity- and market-related reasons, to continue their operations there.

In 1999, when the German owners of a British car manufacturing plant threatened to close it down because of low productivity and operational loss, the government offered millions of pounds in subsidies to help change the owners' mind and save hundreds of jobs in the process.

The quality of the infrastructure in the target country, such as its distribution networks, telecommunications systems, roads and railways, is a crucial factor. Poor physical and institutional infrastructure is one of the factors which, for instance, has made some multinationals cautious when weighing the merits of direct investment in Russia. Factors such as political ideology, religious and other sociocultural dispositions of people, commercial laws, and regulations regarding the environment, health and safety standards, are also usually considered carefully by firms before they decide to set up subsidiaries abroad. Some countries, like Sweden, Germany and Norway, have very stringent environmental regulations which prohibit companies with toxic wastes, such as chemicals firms and nuclear processing plants, to operate on their soil unless they meet certain safety and environmental requirements and standards. But other countries are less particular in this respect. Britain, for instance, has welcomed, and still does to a large extent despite protests by environmental pressure groups, nuclear and other highly toxic industrial wastes from other countries to be reprocessed in its waste-processing plants.

In many countries, especially the industrialised ones, a potential or actual market, rich and discriminating consumers, and a healthy economic atmosphere could be the principal reasons for foreign direct investment.

WHERE AND HOW TO GO

Intertwined with the above-mentioned motives and considerations is the decision as to where to go and what entry mode or modes to choose, such as exporting, franchising, licensing, engaging in cross-border partnerships and joint ventures and setting up wholly-owned subsidiaries – all of which are guided by many considerations. In addition, a company's own core competencies, discussed in the previous chapter, gives it a potential for internationalisation, the realisation of which depends on other internal and external factors.

Take exporting, probably the simplest form of internationalisation and entry mode, for example. The products that the company makes and intends to sell abroad must obviously be of interest to customers abroad. In addition, the image of a company and its reputation in making quality products help create and sustain demands for them. The Hoovers, Mieles, Fords, Toyotas, Toshibas, ICIs and IBMs of this world have little or no problem assuring their global customers of their product quality. Here also what one might call the 'home-country effect' comes into play. A national reputation for quality almost always sells: Persian carpets, Dutch tulips, Scotch whisky, German white goods, American computer software, Japanese electronics gadgets, French wines, Italian fashion. In the same manner, the nations which have earned, rightly or wrongly, adverse reputations in the international economic and political arenas are quite likely to cause potential customers to turn their backs on their domestic firms' products, even if they are of comparable quality and specifications to the nations with a more positive image.

Many third world countries suffer from product image problems, and as a result their companies will have a harder time to sell their products in comparison with their counterparts from more advanced nations, even to their own compatriots. If as a shop assistant in a typical bazaar in Iran or India or a Middle Eastern country you show two identical pairs of jeans, one with a western brand tag and the other with a local make badge, your local customer is highly unlikely to buy the locally-made pair even if its price is a fraction of its western rival. Similarly, the negative image of the so-called political 'pariahs' could damage their domestic companies' chances of internationalisation and limit their scope for expansion to only a few friendly nations. The chances of an otherwise competent Libyan or Sudanese company beating its American or British rivals in the fight to win global customers is very slim indeed. This is of course besides the justice or injustice in branding and pigeon-holing such nations in the first place.

And how about the choice of country or countries to which a firm may wish to export? It is customary nowadays to talk about the global village, but the village is not really all that global. And at any rate it exists, in its limited scope, only for major multinational companies which operate within and between a handful of advanced nations, notably OECD member states, and the more successful emerging economies of Asia and Latin America which account for a large proportion of cross-border trade, partnerships and foreign direct investment. Some central and eastern European countries have only joined the village since the early 1990s, and even then largely as receivers and not givers of investment, products and services.

Some countries are off-limits in internationalisation terms, mainly for political reasons even if an engagement with them might make perfect economic sense to the companies involved. The international community, led by the United States, has boycotted oil-rich Libya and Iraq and natural resource-rich Cuba. Iran, a country with enormous potential, has been shunned since the 1979 revolution by major multinationals in western countries and their allies. Only recently, against the wishes of the United States, some EU and Southeast Asian countries have made overtures to officials of Iran to start political dialogues and business relationships.

Sometimes, the exclusion of certain nations as a market for exported goods or as a venue for direct investment is on human-rights grounds; South Africa under the apartheid regime comes to mind for example, even though there were quite a few major multinationals which ignored the general trend. There is, however, no consistency among nations and companies with regard to human rights and other civil rights as a basis for trade sanctions. Many countries with poor records in this regard, such as China, Indonesia, Myanmar (formerly Burma) and Turkey, continue to receive officially-sanctioned investment, aid, and goods and services, for both civilian and military purposes. Even the Taliban regime in Afghanistan is being directly and indirectly engaged in dialogue by the United States in order to gain access to the oilfields of central Asian countries (*The Economist*, 19 September 1998) which were once a part of the former Soviet Union.

Companies wishing to export to other countries might also face host-country resistance on other political economic grounds. Developing countries which pursue protectionist trade policies and levy tariffs on imported goods often do so in order to help domestic manufacturers. But at times these policies could serve to entice exporters to become foreign direct investors in an attempt to overcome the barriers to entry. It is, however, worth noting that erecting barriers to importation of goods and services from abroad is not unique to developing countries. Japanese and French governments of different political persuasions have systematically used tariff and non-tariff barriers to reduce or prevent the entry of certain products into their countries. The EU member states are still very protective of their domestic agricultural produce market for political reasons, notably as a response to pressures from powerful farm lobbies. In Germany, for example, farmers constitute a major voting bloc in general and local elections.

Even in the United States, which in international negotiations and agreements advocates liberal trade policies, protectionist policies are employed from time to time. In the economic downturn atmosphere of 1998 some industries which were most affected by the crisis and threatened by imports, such as steel, micro-chip, petrochemicals and paper, lobbied the government for introduction of import controls and were duly promised swift action (*The Economist*, 19 September 1998). The so-called 'banana war' between the EU member states, supporting some of their traditional suppliers in their ex-colonies, and the United States, supporting some of its major multinational companies, is but one example of non-liberal trade conducted by some of the world's most vocal champions of liberal trade.

Also worth noting is the fact that certain developing countries, such as Brazil and Mexico, have, largely under pressure from the IMF in return for loans, reduced or brought down many of their import barriers and opened up their markets to foreign goods and services. Mexico, together with the United States and Canada, is also a member of the NAFTA regional agreement according to which trade barriers between members have disappeared.

Exporting, by definition, especially in the case of manufactured products, involves those materials which can be physically moved around in good time before they are rendered unusable. Perishable items, such as freshly-made ready-to-serve fast food, are usually more suitable for other forms of internationalisation, notably franchising and licensing. McDonald's hamburger restaurants and Kentucky Fried Chicken bars are some of the globally well-known examples. However, here also culture and politics play a role.

The Bharatiya Janata Party, which came to power in India in 1998 and was still in charge when the present book went to press, has expressed fears that Indian culture may be eroded by foreign investment in food and drinks, and so is determined to curtail future investment in alcoholic and soft drinks, potato crisps, pizza parlours and the like (*The Economist*, 7 March 1998). In addition, religious beliefs and taboos have to be respected by the franchised outlets if a company is to be allowed entry into a country and accepted by the general public. 'Hamburgers', for instance, cannot contain ham and other pork products in non-secular Muslim and Jewish countries, 'beefburgers' must be beef-free for Hindus.

Foreign direct investment, in the form of both joint ventures and wholly-owned subsidiaries, and indeed the so-called globalisation, has been on the increase in recent decades, building on a trend of wide-and-deep multinationalisation which particularly characterises the twentieth century. A major political force behind a sudden increase in foreign direct investment especially in western Europe by American multinationals in the mid-1940s and 1950s was of course the Marshall Plan. The Marshall Plan accelerated a trend which had already started in the intervening years between the two world wars in the first half of the twentieth century. Western European countries had been devastated by the ravages of the Second World War, and had to be rebuilt to become a powerful counterbalance to the communist Eastern bloc. In addition, these countries needed to shift their manufacturing sector from producing armaments and other war-related products to making commercial and other civilian goods. This required new skills and technologies which American firms were able to provide.

In our own time, especially since the early 1990s, we have seen a remarkable increase in the openness to trade and investment flows in a large part of the world. This has been in part because of the spread of new information technology; partly because of the demise of central planning and the communist model which embodies the ultimate closed-door protectionist ideology; and partly because of the success of the WTO and its predecessor GATT, in getting member nations to agree on a certain measure of liberalisation.

At both national and company levels, decisions to engage in foreign direct investment are influenced by political and cultural factors as well as economic and commercial ones – at the entry stage and once operational within the host country. Some third world countries choose to have foreign investment on a temporary basis, notably in the form of turnkey projects. These nations, although they might need foreign firms for economic reasons, prefer to reduce their dependence on them for long-term political and economic reasons. A limited-life turnkey operation could bring the usual benefits of inward investment such as technical and managerial know-how and employment, but at the same time it will not remain long enough to either dominate the local economy or make itself indispensable for ever.

A variation on such a theme has been employed by Iran in recent years in the form of 'buy-back' projects (see also Chapter 2) to engage foreign multinationals in its oil industry, an industry which has been engulfed by foreign and domestic politics as well as economic considerations since its birth in the late nineteenth century. In fact strategic industries are especially sensitive areas in many developing countries when it comes to foreign investment involvement. Governments in these countries are most reluctant to let go of the control and ownership of such industries, even to pass them on to their own private sector domestic firms, let alone foreign multinationals.

Foreign direct investment among industrialised nations of western Europe and north America and a few other OECD member states are relatively unproblematic. There is virtually no political control over the process. British companies can just as easily set up plants in the USA and American firms in the UK as they can in their resepctive home countries. They are more or less subject to the same laws and regulations in their host country as are their local counterparts. However, many other nations, especially the ex-colonies of today's major economic powers or those which have somehow been manipulated and exploited by such powers in the past, are suspicious of multinational companies from these powers. The East India Company still lives on in the collective memory of Indian people after over two and a half centuries. Certain US companies have in the past been instrumental in furthering their home countries' political goals in Latin America. The involvement of AT&T in the US-supported coup d'état which led to the overthrow of Allende's regime and the coming to power of General Pinochet in Chile in 1973 (Morgan, 1986) is a textbook example of such political interventions.

The situation, however, as Rugman (1998) argues, appears to have changed since those heady days. Nowadays multinational firms have a good record of observing the regulations imposed by governments and international organisations. They appear to be, in any case, too pre-occupied with survival, profitability and growth to interfere in any major way in the social, cultural and other non-economic areas of national activity.

According to Rugman, the nature of triad (US, EU, Japan) based competition faced by these multinational firms limits their ability to pursue political goals since they are forced to concentrate on their ongoing operational efficiency and strategic planning in order to survive. Conflict can arise between foreign firms and government in the arena of international political economy. This relates to the ability of such firms to lobby and otherwise influence the policies of national (and sub-national) governments in areas such as trade, investment, science and technology, and in the administration of these policies by bureaucracies. Yet, even here the interests of international firms have largely centred on their own part of the triad. For example, Japanese multinationals have been mainly concerned to develop competitiveness in Japan and only contribute peripherally to the public policies of the countries in which they have subsidiaries.

This change in the situation may in part be a reason why some previously sceptical countries are now gradually opening up their doors to foreign investors. India, for instance, has, albeit very reluctantly, in the past few years allowed 100 per cent foreign ownership in a limited number of industries. Foreign companies which are on rare occasions able to invest in Iran are allowed to hold up to 49 per cent shares. China and the ex-socialist countries of central and eastern Europe, although on the whole prefering joint ventures to wholly-owned subsidiaries, have allowed some foreign investors to own 100 per cent shares.

However, restrictions on foreign ownership still remains in large parts of the world, including industrialised nations, In Sweden, for instance, foreign investors cannot own more than 40 per cent of a company's equity and are limited to 20 per cent of shareholders' votes. South Korea and Japan have until recently refused permission to foreign companies to own shares above certain percentages in local firms, and have given permission to just a few foreign firms to set up wholly-owned operating units. As Julius (1990) points out, as recently as 1986, only 1 per cent of Japan's assets were owned by foreign-controlled firms, and just 0.4 per cent of its workers were employed by them. This contrasts, for example, with the United States where foreign-controlled firms owned 9 per cent of assets, employed 4 per cent of the workers, and accounted for one-tenth of all sales. In Britain, foreign-controlled firms owned 14 per cent of assets, employed one in seven workers and accounted for one-fifth of all sales. In Germany, foreign-controlled companies owned 17 per cent of assets. It was only after months of meetings, negotiations and threats of retaliation that Americans and western Europeans were able to persuade Japan to open up its market to imports and to allow foreign direct investment.

OPERATING ABROAD

Once a multinational firm is given permission to set up shop, so to speak, in the host country there are domestic requirements which might restrict and even shape its activities including its internal organisational matters, again for political and cultural reasons. Foreign firms may be required to include local people in their top management teams, and to use a certain proportion of local content in the assembly of imported components. They may be asked to build or contribute to the construction of local amenities such as roads, houses for employees, hospital, schools and similar facilities in the areas where the firms are located.

The administrative machinery might be bedevilled with corruption and incompetence. This can force foreign firms, in their efforts to obtain a licence to operate in or deal with a country, to be caught in a complicated web of bureaucratic procedures and paperwork. They may also have to deal with corrupt officials who would manipulate the situation in order to extract commissions from the firms before granting them permission to trade. Once permission is granted the firms have to coexist with these people and procedures for as long as they intend to continue their operations in that country. Not knowing the rules of the game is likely to jeopardise the foreign firms' successful operation and therefore be a source of risk and threat.

Governments might also take actions which are primarily aimed at driving the foreign company out of their country. They could, for example, require foreign firms to pay excessive licence fees and high taxes. Such charges can be increased to the point where making profits is not possible and the company is therefore forced to leave. Foreign firms may not be allowed to repatriate their profits, or may be forced to invest all or a proportion of the profits in specific governmental projects. The firm's employees could be encouraged to go on strike, and consumers asked to boycott its products. All these factors could make life for the foreign firm unbearable to the point of divestment and departure for good. The potential for such government interference is obviously greater for strategic industries such as oil, steel, power stations, arms and weaponry, and high technology, than for non-strategic ones. For instance, a company making shoes is less likely to face hostility from the host government than a firm engaging in oil extraction or running nuclear power stations.

There are also other factors which may make a company prone to such hostile actions: a foreign company might produce a large amount of the host country's GNP; it could be a subsidiary of a powerful multinational which can or even does exert political and economic pressure on the host country; it may have access to and control over export markets. All these could be a source of conflict between the company's goals and the national interests of the host country.

Host-country hostile activities are more often than not carried out against multinationals from western countries in certain developing countries. The reason could be that the latter need technological and managerial know-how and capital from advanced countries in order to build their infrastructure and strategic industries. And at the same time they would ideally want to reduce and/or terminate this dependence as soon as possible. The effect of all this could mean not only the early departure of foreign firms already operating within a country but also a warning, even a deterrent, to prospective direct investors.

The political, economic and cultural factors discussed above serve to limit the reach of multinational enterprises and to challenge their omnipotence. The much talked about globalisation as a result remains a theoretical possibility but not a reality as yet. Most of the largest multinational firms are based in the 'triad' economies of the USA, Europe and Japan, and economic and other constraints mean that they tend to concentrate on their home regions – 443 of the world's largest 500 multinationals come from these areas (Rugman, 1998). For example, the world automobile industry is not truly global; instead, well over 80 per cent of production and sales takes place in each of the three separate triad markets, using inter-bloc networks of suppliers and distributors. The regional nature of the automobile industry is repeated in chemicals, petrochemicals, steel and other major industrial sectors. Thus, the overriding goal is market access on a regional rather than a global basis.

SUMMARY

This chapter has considered some of the major motives for internationalisation of firms, from home-country-related push factors, of both positive and negative nature, to attractions of, and enticement offered by, host countries. It has also been argued that the decision to internationalise is intertwined with how and where to go and that politics has a role to play in the whole process. Political pariahs and economic backwaters cause image problems not only for themselves but also for their otherwise fully 'qualified' domestic firms with international ambitions. Politically-motivated economic sanctions levelled against a nation could and would also exclude its citizens from international markets as potential customers, limiting in the process the internationalisation and globalisation of foreign firms.

Once a foreign firm successfully tackles all the hurdles on its path and enters a host country, there are further factors, mostly politically motivated, which could interfere with its operations. All in all, internationalisation is not a free-for-all option even if the launching pads and the launched companies have all the requirements and qualifications for such an option.

The issue of a foreign firm operating inside a host country will be discussed further in the following chapter.

Part II
Socio-Political Forces and the Management of International Firms

5 Relationships with the External Environment

INTRODUCTION

International firms, like their purely domestic counterparts, meet and have to cope with external socio-political challenges thrown at them, except that these are far more complex and varied because of the complex and varied 'world' in which they operate. The intensity of these challenges, however, depends on the degree of internationalisation of the companies concerned – the deeper and wider their wings spread, the more complex their external environment and the more intense the challenges they have to face. For a single-nation firm with no direct international interest, the host-country characteristics are virtually irrelevant, if not non-existent. As a firm becomes engaged in international activities, from import/export to foreign direct investment, it becomes more deeply involved with foreign people and institutions as customers, business partners, suppliers and employees; its fate becomes more and more entwined with theirs, and its tasks more and more challenging. Table 5.1 illustrates this point.

Table 5.1   Multinational firms and host nations

Degree of internationalisation	Relevance of host country sociocultural and political economic characteristics
Domestic single-nation firm with no foreign interests	Nil
Single-nation firm with import/export activities	Low to moderate
Multinational firm with franchising and licensing activities	Moderate to high
Multinational firm with manufacturing and/or service units abroad	High
'Global' firm with various business activities in most parts of the world	High

Source: Adapted from Tayeb (1996).

The present chapter identifies major parts of what is, in effect, a patchwork context within which international firms operate: governments, suppliers, customers, partners, all with different values, preferences, policies and priorities. International firms not only have to respond to the challenges posed by this context; they also help shape it in some ways. The focus of the discussions which follow will be on the host(s) rather than the home of the firms, as it is the host-related factors which distinguish the external context of a multinational firm from its single-nation counterparts.

GETTING TO THE HOST COUNTRY

For exporting companies, the first hurdle to get through is to manufacture the kind of products that some foreign customers want, or could be persuaded, to buy in the first place. Here cultural tastes and preferences play a significant part. Some people, like the majority of the British, like small cars, for instance, while their American counterparts prefer big ones. Petrol prices, car tax, income, width of the roads, population density, and size of the country as a whole might of course have something to do with this difference of tastes, but that is how, in part at least, tastes and preferences are formed and sustained over time.

Religious habits and taboos might prevent some products from being consumed in large enough numbers to make exporting to certain countries viable. The manufacturers of pork sausages, for example, may find difficulties in finding customers in Israel and many Muslim countries. Religious and cultural factors, as was mentioned in the previous chapter, could also determine the acceptability or desirability of the products of foreign franchised and licensed outlets especially in the fast food sector. A touch of hot spice might meet with the approval of those nations which prefer spicy foods, and for the ecologically conscious 'fried chickens' must be of the free-range kind.

Also important is whether or not the information about the company's products can flow freely across borders and without distortion. Merely to pose such a question might cause some readers' eyebrows to rise. But it is a fact of life that in many countries, especially those with hostile attitudes towards certain other nations, or those with protected economies, a vast majority of ordinary people do not really know what is available beyond what they are allowed to be exposed to. In Cuba, for instance, there are restrictions on private enterprises, a carpenter can only make things if his customer brings along the piece of wood which he wants to be converted to a bookshelf (*The Economist*, 26 September, 1998). What chances are there for the carpenter to use or even to know about the quality of Scandinavian pine wood? This is in sharp contrast to the situation in the liberal-minded United Kingdom where the same product is imported and extensively used by furniture makers.

Then there is the role of government in the mechanics as well as the principle of trade with foreign importers or exporters. The views and policies of governments, which issue export or import permits, regarding some commodities and products affect their decisions to grant or withhold such permits. The current British government, in office since 1997, for instance, has adopted an ethical foreign policy according to which sales of arms to certain nations with poor human-rights records are not permitted.

Governments could also set in place severe restrictions or a total ban on the export of certain commodities such as works of art and antiques, especially in countries which in the past, notably in the nineteenth century, have lost many of their national treasures thanks to over-zealous foreign explorers and archaeologists. The ordinary people's views on such matters may also influence their government. In the United Kingdom, for example, there is almost always an outcry from the public whenever a valuable and nationally cherished painting is sold to a foreign bidder. Under such pressures the government usually places a temporary export ban on the object concerned allowing time for local enthusiasts and museums to raise money to buy it back for the nation.

As for the run of the mill consumer and capital goods, in liberalminded countries the role of government is to encourage exports and imports and to enable the free flow of goods and services to and from their country. Permissions are usually issued subject to health, safety and other non-political conditions, with some exceptions regarding certain targeted 'unfriendly' nations. Exporters may freely negotiate with their local distributors, sales agents and so on and work out the details without interference from their respective governments. But in many countries, such as China, India and most other developing nations, the host government representatives are very much a part of the negotiation process at the outset, and foreign exporters can only begin the process by talking to them first, then continuing the rest of the negotiations and later their operations under their shadow.

The situation can become more complicated and tricky when dealing with bureaucratic and/or corrupt officials who want their share of the 'proceeds' before granting entry permission. Corruption is, of course, neither limited to government officials nor to business matters. In any case, international companies are becoming increasingly conscious of the ethical side of their business (see for instance Taka and Foglia, 1994; Stajkovic and Luthans, 1997), and many have devised ethical policies to cover their interface activities, such as negotiations and securing contracts; their operations, such as the location in which they wish to invest or to which they might export their products; and their human resources, such as age, minimum wage and working conditions.

Negotiations with both government representatives and business partners also have a cultural dimension. Misunderstandings of other people's points of view purely because of cultural reasons can easily terminate prematurely an otherwise successful process. The issue goes far beyond a knowledge (or lack of it) of one's interlocutors' language. It is so easy for a person from one cultural grouping to miss the underlying meanings and intentions which lie behind what someone from a different culture might say or do. As Jankowicz (1994) points out, some people tend to underestimate the difficulties involved in the creation of shared understanding and scarcely recognise the issue of cultural differences. Hall and Hall's (1990) concepts of high and low contexts point to a very significant and crucial issue in this regard. In high-context nations there are far more hidden, unspoken and taken-for-granted meanings when people communicate with one another than in low-context cultures. Unless one is familiar with these hidden meanings, crosscultural business negotiations may be awkward affairs.

The manner in which information exchange and communication are structured in negotiations and other business encounters can also reflect the high and low contexts. For example, high-context people such as the Japanese are rather slow getting to the point and do not expect to have to be very specific even when they do. They talk around the point. They think that intelligent human beings should be able to discover the point of a discourse from the context, which they are careful to provide. In contrast, low-context people are fast in getting to the point, they tend to over-inform and are much more direct in delivering their message (Hall, 1989).

The use of humour and proverbial expressions and sayings in cross-cultural communications and negotiations is particularly risky as they relate to and reflect a great deal of the cultural and historical heritage of the native speakers, all or some of which might be unknown to foreigners. The meaning of 'British Prime Minister is batting for Britain in EU negotiations' is totally lost to all except a few cricket-loving nations. This sort of cultural barrier can even exist within a nation across generations or even political ideologies. Recently a British member of parliament with left-leaning political views said that when he hears the phrase 'cool Britannia' he thinks of old-age pensioners who suffer from hypo-thermia. Even more risky is the use of such expressions by a non-native person while speaking to native negotiating partners. Incorrect applica-tion can and does lead to misunderstandings and embarrassment.

In addition, there is of course body language and other mannerisms. In one culture, calling partners by their first names and putting one's feet on the coffee table may be intended to signal trust and friendliness to them; the partners, if from a different culture, may interpret these gestures as carelessness and downright rudeness. In some cultures, like India and some Arab countries, maintaining a close physical distance to the person you speak with is a sign of friendship and trust. In some others, such as Japan and Britain, people are very particular in keeping a cer-tain distance. In many western countries, nowadays, if people of the same sex hold hands in public they are generally assumed to be gays/ lesbians; in many eastern countries this only implies friendship and politeness, nothing more.

In many parts of the world an encounter with someone from a differ-ent culture in both professional and leisure contexts often arouses com-plex and totally baseless emotions, such as fear, anxiety, mistrust and suspicion, and even amusement. The mere fact that someone does not have a command of one's language or maybe speak it fluently but with an unfamiliar accent could cause one to doubt that person's compet-ence or ability to grasp complicated issues. To build trust and confid-ence in one's negotiating partners takes time. And in most crosscultural international negotiations time is one of the factors which is not always in ample supply, especially when partners meet in airport lounges in between their professional trips.

Also, foreign partners not only speak languages other than one's own, they also have a tendency, for cultural reasons, to think in differ-ent ways and to have different priorities in the ways in which they do business (Hagen, 1988). There are in every culture logical, accepted and practised 'rules of the game', evolved over time in response to its own specific sets of problems and circumstances. In most Arab coun-tries, for example, business negotiations are conducted through medi-ators, agents and go-betweens, rooted in their time-honoured tribal social system (Cunnigham and Sarayrah, 1993), some of whom might demand, quite legally according to their customs, commissions for the services rendered (Solberg, 1998). In some cultures, people involved in business deals would like to build up personal relationships with and establish the trustworthiness of their trade counterparts before going on to engage in business contracts and dealings with them. In other cultures, business negotiators would prefer to get down to the nitty-gritty of the deals and contracts straightaway, relying heavily on the legal rights and obligations clauses included therein to safeguard their interests.

Altany (1989), comparing American business people with their European counterparts, points out that Americans often feel that the European practice of meticulously cultivating personal relationships with business associates hampers the expedient conduct of business. They argue that time is money and the Europeans waste time. But to the Europeans, trust and long-term commitment – not legal contracts and short-term gains – are the heart and soul of a solid business relationship. And the European approach, slower though it is, usually leads to longer and stronger business alliances. In addition, it is worth noting that, as Macquin and Rouzies (1998) argue, negotiators do not always negotiate with someone from their own culture in the same way they do with someone from another culture. In other words, knowing how Chinese people negotiate with each other, for instance, will not give negotiating teams from other cultures much help in predicting how the Chinese will negotiate with *them*.

In a case study that the present author conducted in the Scottish subsidiary of an American multinational company (Tayeb, 1998), the frustration caused by such rules of the game was very clear. At the time of the research fieldwork in 1997 the Scottish plant was in the process of negotiations with would-be Chinese partners to enter into a joint venture and set up a manufacturing plant in China. The company's negotiating team was made up of five people with expertise in marketing, manufacturing, product, law and business development in China, among others. Two members of the team were also fluent Mandarin speakers.

The negotiations were progressing at a very slow pace, a pace determined by the Chinese partners. When the team first went to China, the expatriates from the then parent company already posted there warned the team of what they might expect in this regard:

> The Chinese will move at the speed they want to move at, they probably don't have all that much in the way of concern for schedule. Time isn't of the essence, it's more the quality of the discussion or the quality of the exchange. And the faster that we tried to go the more it would cost us to do it. We would have to give up more and more and more until we're probably losing money on the deal.

The team started the negotiations in Beijing in March 1995 and months later they had still a long way to go. Typically, when negotiators reached a certain position, the Chinese partners would say they must now go back to the ministries that supported them. They would then come back and say that, for instance, the deal was unacceptable, and the whole process had to start all over again. Or they might change team members on their side because, for example, the government ministries did not feel they were doing as good a job as they might. This meant that the Scottish negotiating team had to get their side of the argument over to these new people. And the seemingly endless circle would commence again.

INSIDE THE HOST COUNTRY

Once a foreign company, whether as exporter or locally-based producer and provider of services, has crossed the entry barriers and is operational inside the host country, there are other challenges to face.

Relation with customers

Advertising and marketing of products and services is one such challenge. Various nations vary in the form and extent of seller–customer communication channels they can support and sustain. The level of technological and economic advancement is an important factor here. So are norms, customs and socially-acceptable codes of conduct, especially with regard to the content and style of commercial messages sent out to potential customers.

A high level of literacy and a widespread habit of reading newspapers and magazines among a population could make the written press a suitable vehicle for advertising. Similarly, the appropriateness of radio, television and the Internet as advertising channels depends on the degree of accessibility of such media to the population. In many parts of the world the scope and reach of these mass communication media are, for reasons such as inadequate technological infrastructure or generally low levels of income, limited. Sometimes, for political reasons, there are government restrictions on the use of such media for private enterprise and commercial purposes. In addition, the Internet is in many countries either out of reach of many private citizens or heavily controlled and monitored by officials. In these circumstances foreign companies might have to either follow their local counterparts' examples, or devise other legal and ingenious ways to get their message across.

What can or cannot be consumed by the general public or advertised in certain public media may also be subject to government policies on health, religious and social grounds. Consumption and advertising of alcoholic drinks in many Muslim countries are forbidden; in some countries, such as the United Kingdom, advertising of tobacco products on radio and television, because of their wide use in homes, are banned. In multiracial, multiethnic societies there may be legal as well as social restrictions and prohibitions on the use of anti-racial language and images in advertising. Marketing devices such as market research and customer surveys may also have limited benefits in countries with poor infrastructure and generally low literacy rates. Telephone surveys and advertising can in many cases irritate people, specially if one does not quite know their culturally-rooted sensitivities to certain questions and issues. A telephone survey about contraceptives or women's hygiene products, for instance, might offend some people's respect for privacy and maintaining inhibitions.

Retail outlets where the imported as well as locally-made goods end up being offered to customers may also follow socially-desirable patterns. In many Middle Eastern and Asian countries, bazaars and small shops are traditionally used as outlets. Supermarkets and department stores, while they are increasingly seen in some of these countries, are not in such numbers and ubiquitous states as one can observe in some other parts of the world, say, the United States and Britain, with their so-called doughnut effect – large shopping centres built in the outskirts of towns and cities and customers taken away from their town-centre precincts.

Other retail business customs such as shopping days and opening hours are again different in various countries, depending on their specific traditions. In many western and other five-day working-week nations, Saturdays are usually shopping days; in some Christian countries shops are closed on Sundays, whereas in some like Scotland there are no restrictions in this regard. In Israel, a Jewish state, Saturday is the Sabbath; in Muslim countries, Friday is the day of rest and shops are usually closed, especially in the afternoon. In some of these countries the five-day working-week habit does not exist (many people usually work seven days a week, with perhaps one afternoon off); also there is usually no specific day of the week when people do the bulk of their shopping. In many western countries opening hours for shops are restricted either voluntarily or by law, except perhaps for the small so-called 'corner' shops in the neighbourhood. In many eastern and more traditional nations shops are open for as long as people like to shop, usually until late into the night.

The amount of adaptation of the original format that will be necessary and the accuracy of information about local retail locations are not easily achievable, as examples cited by Horovitz and Kumar (1998) demonstrate. The French retails chain Galeries Lafayette failed in New York and Singapore because it was not sufficiently different from local department stores. Ikea, when it opened in the US, underestimated the amount of product adaptation necessary for American homes as well as the reaction speed of cheaper competitors. Virgin in France took too large a floor space outside Paris to make it profitable. By contrast, Spar, a voluntary chain of independent retailers, operates successfully six different formats to suit different local conditions: 24-hour urban stores; neighbourhood stores in small towns and villages; Spar markets (up to 400 square metres); supermarkets (up to 1000 square metres); hypermarkets Euro (up to 2800 square metres); and InterSpar (above 5000 square metres).

McDonald's has similar adaptability policies. According to Watson (1998), McDonald's restaurants situated in East Asia, indeed as elsewhere, are all run by locals. And far from accepting the same McDonald's that Americans do, Asian consumers gradually twist McDonald's to their own purposes. Rather than being fast, efficient take-out eating places, many McDonald's restaurants are more akin to Seattle coffee houses – places to hang out for the young. In several places, McDonald's has gone so native that many of its customers do not realise it is American. In China, one of McDonald's appeals is the fact that its menu is very limited; there is no danger of losing face because the table next door orders a more expensive dish. As Watson concludes, people come for the experience not the product; and they make sure that it is their experience – not one foisted upon them by an American juggernaut.

Another culturally-rooted custom affecting the retailing of goods is of course haggling over prices. In many traditional societies, prices shown on the labels are only the starting points and both customers and sellers get away with the eventual prices that their bargaining prowess, shrewdness and stamina can help them to exact from one another. In less traditional western societies such rules of games do not exist, and haggling in fact is institutionalised through market forces at the wholesale levels rather than through end-customers' and retail-sellers' direct one-to-one interventions.

Politics also has a role to play here. In many developing economies, especially those with acute poverty and similar social problems, essential food items such as bread and rice are sold at fixed low prices or are heavily subsidised for targeted groups through special coupons and vouchers. In countries which are still run on communist models or those with socialist and protectionist leanings, price fixing and subsidisation go far beyond essential food products. In many capitalist societies there are government appointed regulators who monitor the quality as well as the price of goods and services provided by monopolies or near-monopolies, especially in utilities and communication sectors.

Sale by mail order is gaining popularity especially in western Europe and north America. But such a style of selling may be a long way from being accepted or adopted in many other countries. Remote sale, apart from a widespread use of credit cards and mutual trust between unseen sellers and buyers as a precondition, also presupposes a strong legal and insurance infrastructure to ensure a proper conduct of business transactions by the two sides. This type of financial and legal infrastructure is either inadequate or totally lacking in many countries; there may also be culturally-rooted mistrust and misgivings regarding such remote transactions.

The use of credit cards in India, for example, although it has been growing in recent years, involves only a relatively small number of people. In 1998, of an estimated 30 million adults who were eligible only three million had a card (*The Economist*, 5 December 1998). Most Indians prefer cash, partly because it leaves no trace – the government added credit cards to the list of assets for which owners must file a tax return in 1998. Major foreign banks which issue credit cards also have the disadvantage of being relatively unknown in the retail business, particularly in smaller Indian cities. But even if the banks win new customers, they will run new risks. For instance, they have no way of checking if a customer has defaulted on a card issued by another bank; the credit information available is inadequate and often wrong. India's legal system also offers little help; some banks hire agents to collect payments from difficult customers. This can prove embarrassing – as one large British bank discovered when a court in Mumbai (formerly Bombay) censured it for 'roughing up' a defaulting customer (*The Economist*, 5 December 1998).

In Germany, where there are legal and other institutional infrastructures to support remote exchanges of goods and money, mail-order retailers are still reluctant to accept credit cards. The German Quelle Schickedanz is one of Europe's largest catalogue retailers. It is a business built on trust, where customers can 'test' a product for 14 days before deciding whether to keep it. If they want it, they're billed and can pay by cheque, cash or as a direct debit to their bank account, but no credit cards or no smart cards are allowed (*Time*, 30 November 1998).

The Internet is the latest retail outlet but has encountered a mixed reception in many places for technical, cultural and cost-related reasons. American consumers, for example, have embraced the Internet as an alternative mail-order shopping venue with far more enthusiasm than their European counterparts. According to a report by Jupiter Communications cited in *Time* (30 November 1998, pp. 51–3), US shoppers were expected to spend $2.3 billion surfing for products and services available through retailers' websites on the Internet in the run up to the 1998 Christmas holidays. European consumers were estimated to spend roughly 5 per cent of that figure. According to the Organisation for Economic Cooperation and Development (OECD), cited in the same source, 80 per cent of the $26 billion global e-commerce market is within the USA, western Europe's share is just 10 per cent. The reasons why Europe trails the USA so badly in e-commerce are myriad, but the cost of going online is a major culprit. The slow pace of telecommunications deregulation and a resulting lack of competition have kept connection costs much higher in Europe than in the USA.

Europe's telecommunications sector can also be blamed for not making up-to-date technology like cable modem access and fibre-optic lines widely available to consumers. Transmission bandwidths across much of Europe are insufficient, which means Internet connections on the continent are slower than in the USA forcing people to remain online longer, further running up phone charges. The high price of computers in Europe relative to the USA is another reason why Internet usage in Europe is lower than in the USA.

European consumer habits do not help either. As the OECD notes, continental shoppers are less fond of buying goods from afar than their American cousins, and European mail-order sales on a per capita basis, for example, are less than half those in the USA. Europeans like to see what they are buying and to feel the product. Also, as mentioned earlier, in many European countries credit cards, useful in mail-order transactions, are not popular.

Relations with suppliers

Since the spectacular economic performance of Japan in the mid-twentieth century which propelled the country into the ranks of highly advanced societies, any discussion of producer–supplier relationships within a crosscultural context brings to mind the Japanese system of just-in-time. The just-in-time method of production involves a finely tuned scheduling system where stocks are supplied only when needed, and work in progress is closely controlled. The system also encourages a modular organisation of work where members of a team are responsible for the completion of any one stage in the production process. The system is supported both by cultural and non-cultural characteristics of Japanese society.

One of the major features of Japanese industrial structure, which lies behind the just-in-time process of production, is the subcontracting relationship which exists between large and small firms. This relationship spreads down a tiered structure, with the principal firm at the apex, followed by a small number of large subcontracting firms, then a tier consisting of a large number of smaller firms, and so forth. The number of tiers in each set of relationships could be as large as seven or eight. Strictly speaking, the subcontracting relationship between large and small firms in Japan has nothing to do with Japanese national culture (in its narrow sense). But the successful implementation of the just-in-time practice depends heavily on the effective operation of such a relationship, which is based on trust, cultivated over a long period of time, and is congruent with the Japanese national character.

Further, the success of modular production as a prerequisite for the operation of just-in-time is dependent on a social organisation for the production process intended to make workers feel obliged to contribute to the economic performance of the enterprise and to identify with its competitive success (Turnbull, 1986). The Japanese are clearly masters at fostering this sense of obligation, built probably on their group orientation and sense of cooperation with others in a team setting, again rooted in their national culture.

Just-in-time, when it was initially imported along with some other Japanese management practices to many western nations, had a qualified success and in some cases failed totally. In the early 1980s a Japanese car manufacturing firm established a subsidiary in the north-east of England. From the beginning the Japanese senior managers expected their suppliers to honour their obligations not only in terms of the quality of the goods delivered but also the delivery time, which was so crucial to the proper application of their production methods. The Japanese managers who were interviewed in a number of television and radio news programmes used to complain that time-keeping was a serious problem as far as some of their local suppliers were concerned. This does not of course mean that prior to the arrival of Japanese companies the British firms suffered from their suppliers' rather relaxed time-keeping. Rather, the local firms knew the rules of the game and would factor it into their calculations and production schedules. But the newcomers were not familiar with the situation and therefore experienced frustrations in the early years of their operation in the UK.

Nearly two decades later the situation has changed somewhat. In a series of case studies of Scottish manufacturing companies conducted by the present author (Tayeb, 1999b), she found that one of them had decided to reorganise its production processes so as to take advantage of just-in-time. The company had succeeded in doing so thanks mainly to a mutually trusting relationship that it had developed over time with the suppliers of its raw materials, as well as retraining its in-house workforce.

Apart from good will and trust, just-in-time also presupposes a reliable overall infrastructure to facilitate quick flow of information and communication between the producers and the suppliers and ensure the prompt delivery of semi-processed and raw materials. As was discussed in previous chapters, this is not the case everywhere, and as a result multinational companies operating in various countries may have to adapt to local distribution networks and ways of doing things. In the process, they also have to forego certain advantages that systems such as just-in-time could bring to them.

Relationships with societal institutions

Some international firms, especially those which have spread wide and deep in their operation and geographical coverage, are quite powerful. Their budgets sometimes surpass those of many nations. But these companies are at the same time subject to rules and regulations of the countries with which they have business relations. The ultimate authority as to how business activities should be conducted within a country's boundaries, and indeed in the international arena, rests with the sovereign states either individually or in conjunction with others, such as the European Union.

As mentioned in an earlier chapter, some nations have relatively hands-off policies as far as business laws are concerned. The limits beyond which firms, domestic and foreign alike, cannot venture are specified and within those limits the firms are free to pursue their legitimate commercial interests. But there are other countries where detailed rules and laws cover anything from permission and license to operate, to social responsibility, mandatory recognition of trade unions, workers' participation and other aspects of human-resource management. In France, for instance, many companies, especially the large ones, are required to spend a certain percentage of their annual turnover on employee training. In the United Kingdom, under a new law, the management has to recognise trade unions as representatives of their employees if a majority of them demands it.

In some countries like Germany and Norway, regulations regarding environmental considerations, such as the preservation and sustainable use of forests and permissible emission levels, are far more stringent than in their fellow European states such as Portugal and Greece, and certainly more so than in many developing nations. This in a way reflects the general socio-political culture of the nations concerned. The awareness of people of ecological issues, which could in turn be channelled through pressure groups and direct democratic participation on to the statute book, depends to a large extent on the degree of freedom of speech and information and also of activities by pressure groups. In some countries, pressure groups are free to operate and exert power and influence through direct and indirect actions on companies and legislators; in some nations such groups are either restricted or nonexistent as a meaningful force.

In some nations the duties and responsibilities of commercial firms towards the community at large are far more narrowly defined than in others. In nations with a large private sector and a widespread general public share ownership pattern, the business organisations' accountability and responsibility are primarily to their shareholders, notwithstanding a minimum regard for the social consequences of their activities. In nations with different institutional arrangements, such as a large public sector and a higher emphasis on stakeholders' as opposed to shareholders' rights, the social responsibilities of companies might take a deeper and wider form. International firms therefore are confronted with a patchwork of laws, regulations, pressures and norms. And more often than not they have to adapt to these rather than try to change them, because of the superiority of sovereign states within their territories.

There are, however, indirect and more subtle ways in which a foreign firm can leave an imprint, albeit perhaps not always too deep, on the host-country's society, as testified by evidence such as that provided by Ritzer (1996) and Watson (1998). Watson, for instance, produces a long list of things that McDonald's has helped change in Asia, including children's birthdays (previously uncelebrated in many places; now hosted by 'Uncle' and 'Aunt' McDonald), queuing in Hong Kong (previously a scrum; now more likely to be in a line), the way that Japanese eat their food (previously always sitting down; now more likely to be standing up); and even smiling at strangers (previously close to an insult in China, now, in McDonald's at least, a sign of good service).

Moreover, at a different level, successful foreign firms, with or without operating plants and units in the host country, are often looked up to as role models by their local counterparts. As Mirza (1998) points out, multinational firms could take with them their business and industry culture to their overseas subsidiaries, and by implication, expose the locals to it. The success of such cross-border adoptions and transfers are however mixed (Oliver and Davies, 1990; Oliver and Wilkinson, 1992; Osterman, 1994; Tayeb, 1994; Shadur *et al.*, 1995; Roney, 1997). Local sociocultural and political-economic conditions and the level of technological advancement can play a significant role in such adoptions by both company's own affiliates and local firms. As a result, the extent to which local subsidiaries accept and implement a parent company's policies and strategies and adopt its ways of doing things varies from subsidiary to subsidiary (Tayeb, 1998), and, as was discussed in earlier chapters, the extent to which local firms can learn from foreigners varies from nation to nation.

SUMMARY

As a part of the entry process, international firms disseminate information about their goods and services to their potential foreign customers through advertising in the international media or international versions of 'word of mouth', and, in the next step, engage in negotiations with governments and business partners to gain entry as exporters or locally-based investors. The cultural and political context of such entry stages and processes have been discussed in this chapter.

We have also explored the effect of the socio-political characteristics of the host country on the process and nature of the network of relationships that a foreign company establishes with its local customers, business partners and suppliers and the ways in which it can use the available media to publicise its wares. In the process, it has been argued, the foreign firm might influence, to some extent, the local people's ways of doing business or even their non-business habits. But it was also stressed that culturally-rooted taken-for-granted assumptions and values, built up over centuries, are too resilient and resistant to change to be more than just scratched on the surface. In addition, since locals know their way around their own home better than foreigners and know better how to get things done, the foreign firm may in fact end up learning a great deal from their local counterparts – more on this in chapter 6.

6 Strategic Development

INTRODUCTION

Brooke (1996, p. 33) defines corporate strategy as 'determining a sense of direction, a set of objectives, for a company and appropriate routes in order to achieve the objectives [which]...do not have to be articulated or committed to a carefully thought-out document'. Clearly, the commercial environment and the broader context within which a firm operates, as well as its internal core competencies, are an influential factor in such a fluid process. Further, corporate strategy and its development can be considered both with respect to the general issues which are relevant to most firms, and also those which concern a decision to expand beyond national boundaries and go international. These issues have of course received extensive attention by researchers writing within strategic management and international business disciplines, especially from the economics angle. Here the implications of sociocultural factors for strategic decisions are explored.

GOAL-SETTING

The most significant strategic decision that a company makes concerns its goals, which in most cases, especially in the private sector in capitalist economies, is to make profit. Many other objectives, such as growth, market share, competitive edge, innovation and so on are set to achieve the original goal. However, as we saw in Chapter 3, such a model of company goals is very limited and cannot fully explain a commercial firm's behaviour in this respect around the world.

The reason lies in part in the fact that there is more than one model of a capitalist political economic system, caused by the diversity of nation-specific socioeconomic institutions which underlie such a system (Crouch and Streeck, 1997). Dore's (1997, pp. 19–20) classification of the ways in which the nature of the private-sector business firm in capitalist societies is viewed is instructive. He distinguishes four positions in this regard: property view; entity/community view (two sub-versions); and arena view:

- According to the *property view*, which is the dominant one among business practitioners in the Anglo-Saxon world, a company is an entity set up by its capital-providing members to further their own material interests. The managers are their agents with a duty to give priority to that shareholder interest, and the careful buying of the best labour as cheaply as they can is as much part of their duty as getting the best bargain out of their suppliers of raw materials.
- The *entity/community view* sees the company as something like a nation, and, thus reified, is seen as an entity which transcends the participating work life of the individuals involved. Further, this entity is at any one time concretely embodied in a particular set of people who, as in a nation, constitute a community, tied together by bonds of mutual interest in the community's fate, obligations of cooperation and trust, the sharing of similar risks. Within this view, a distinction can be made between the *managerial community view* and the *employee community view*. The latter implies that the shareholders are just one of the groups of outsiders who have to be taken into account for the community to survive and prosper.
- In the *arena view*, the firm is seen as an area in which individuals or groups of individuals – groups usually referred to as 'stakeholders' – make, often implicit, contracts of various kinds. The organisation of a firm can be 'dissolved' into a network of contracts; productive activities are pursued as the fulfilment of bargains motivated exclusively by individual self-interest.

Given the above classification, Dore argues that the property view is dominant in the UK and the USA, with some deviation towards the management community view. In contrast, the dominant model in Japan corresponds to the employee community view, that is the employee version of the entity/community view.

Yoshimori (1995) makes similar comments on UK, US, German, French and Japanese companies with regard to their main interest groups. In the United States and the UK, he notes, companies predominantly follow a 'monistic' approach, in which the firm is perceived as the private property of its shareholders. In Germany and to some extent France, a 'dualistic' outlook is dominant, that is a premium is placed on shareholders' interests, but those of the employees are also important. Japanese firms take a 'pluralistic' view, according to which the company belongs to all stakeholders, with the employees' interest taking precedence.

One can take Dore's and Yoshimori's arguments further and explore some of the cultural and institutional roots of these contrasting views which are prevalent in various nations. Culturally, American and British peoples are highly individualistic. For them the 'self' stands in the centre of one's world. For instance, with regard to the English, who form by far the largest proportion of the UK population, Macfarlane (1978), having examined various historical documents, argues that 'the majority of people in England from at least the thirteenth century were rampant individualists, highly mobile both geographically and socially, economically "rational", market-oriented and acquisitive, and ego-centred in kinship and social life' (p. 163), and from the thirteenth century onwards 'it is not possible to find a time when an Englishman did not stand alone. Symbolised and shaped by his ego-centred kinship system, he stood at the centre of his world' (p. 196).

In the UK in general, a person's loyalty is to him/herself and his or her nuclear family only. In other words, their in-group is small and does not go beyond their immediate family and perhaps a few close relatives and friends. Personal interests generally take precedence over group interests, and one fights for one's views to be heard and taken note of. Americans too are independent and individualistic, place a high value on freedom and believe that individuals can shape and control their own destinies. They pride themselves on being fiercely individualistic (Bakhtari, 1995). In this connection Hall (1989) also argues that the Americans are much more concerned with their own careers and personal success than about the welfare of the organisation for which they work or the group to which they belong.

As shareholders, one can reasonably safely argue, the company which the British and Americans are part-owners of is not a part of their in-group; rather it is a means to further their personal financial interests. It is well-known, especially in the USA, that people (as shareholders) are rich but the companies they own are poor, having been thoroughly milked by them.

In Japan, by contrast, a different set of cultural and economic factors has set them on to a direction opposite to the one taken by their American and British counterparts. Their collectivist culture emphasises group interests rather than those of the individual, and consensus and harmony take precedence over open conflicts between the various parties involved. It appears that a person's in-group not only includes his or her family and close friends and relatives, but also his or her workplace. Moreover, as we saw in Chapter 3, the industrial structure and economic institutions of the country favours concentrated share ownership in the hands of a few stakeholders, as opposed to a widespread public ownership pattern. This gives Japanese companies the luxury of long-term financial support within their network of relationships with banks and other financial institutions. As a result, the companies' goals can be set with a view to achieving long-term growth and a larger market share, and fighting off competitors, rather than paying dividends to shareholders and fighting off hostile takeovers. Profits are ploughed back into the company rather than distributed to numerous share-holders in return for their loyalty. In sharp contrast to the USA, Japanese companies are arguably rich but the people of Japan are relatively poor.

Also, as was discussed in Chapter 3, in many parts of the world, especially developing countries, the scope of organisational goals spills over into the community at large. A multinational company with operations in culturally and economically-diverse locations will have to be responsive to the host nation's 'definition' of organisational goals, and factor in whatever else apart from making profit is expected of it. In the flip-side to what was discussed in Chapter 5 regarding foreign firms being role models for local counterparts, there are occasions, in this case goal-setting, where the foreign firm could follow the examples of the local firm. If the local manager takes on the role of social worker and community figurehead in addition to his internal organisational responsibilities, the foreign manager may find it uncomfortable, or even unacceptable, to stay aloof and detached, preoccupied with making profit and increasing market share alone.

EXPANSION ABROAD

Setting strategies in multinational companies, much as single-nation ones, takes place in the light of the companies' internal resources and external opportunities, factors which are much more complicated and sometimes unpredictable in firms with operations in various nations. Production technology, the level of workforce skills, managerial know-how and financial resources are some of the major internal factors which would guide a firm's strategies and future capabilities.

Although the first of these can be provided by the parent company, its operationalisation depends on the local workforce, the quality of which is uneven across nations. It also depends on the ability of the parent company to help the local employees along by training and even direct control if need be, which might not be plain sailing. There could, for instance, be resistance by the host-country employees to direct control from the centre, or even cultural resistance to the parent company's presumption of superiority of their ways of doing things over those of the locals. Further, the training of employees might also in most cases involve a process of unlearning of unwanted previous skills and work attitudes, the situation experienced by many multinational firms now operating in ex-communist countries. This requires a different kind of understanding and competency on the part of the parent company management team, such as sensitivity to and respect for local culture, views and beliefs.

The multifaceted environment within which the multinational firm operates may offer both opportunities and risks, information about which may not be easily available, especially in developing nations. Data-gathering procedures regarding economic and business activities are not standardised around the world and cannot all be considered as reliable. In most countries such data are collected by government agencies and may well go through a 'cleansing' filter before being made available to interested parties. Moreover, some of the information available, such as it is, may not be accessible to foreign firms for legal and security reasons. Then there is the problem of interpretation of locally gathered information by a foreign firm unfamiliar with contextual nuances. Also, sometimes valuable information could be passed on from a local firm to another local firm in informal networks of connections from which a foreign firm may well be excluded.

Keiretsu groupings in Japan are a formidable barrier to entry for foreign firms with strategic expansion plans to locate in that country. The formal and informal networks among the member firms, from suppliers to banks and other providers of capital, shareholders, wholesalers and retailers, exclude a foreign body which by implication is not an organic part of these networks and cannot be transplanted there. Such problems affect not only a firm's strategic decision to expand its operation abroad, but also its on-going strategies and functions once it is located in the host country. Foreigners have to operate alongside these networks and devise ways of dealing with the competitive advantage that such groupings provide for the insiders, the local firms.

It is perhaps because of these sorts of difficulties that some researchers have argued that multinational firms expand to other countries if there are cultural affinities between the home and host countries – the so-called cultural distance and psychic distance theories of internationalisation. Psychic distance, defined as factors preventing or disturbing the flows of information between firms and markets, is argued to be of the utmost importance to international operations. Examples of such factors coming under the above definition are: differences in language, culture, political systems, level of education and level of industrial developments. Companies are assumed to venture out into nations which are close to their home country in terms of psychic distance and accumulate experience there, before moving into economies further afield (see for example Beckermann, 1956; Johanson and Wiedersheim-Paul, 1975; Hallén and Wiedersheim-Paul, 1979). Building on this, Nordström and Vahlne (1992) have developed a 'cultural distance' index, which in comparison with the psychic distance, in their view, captured different but overlapping phenomena.

Kogut and Singh (1988), relying largely on Hofstede's (1980) research, quantified cultural distance between countries. They further argued that one consideration on the part of a parent company to internationalise is the ability of the firm to manage the local operations of its subsidiary. This ability may in turn be influenced by two considerations, the absolute cultural attitudes towards uncertainty-avoidance and the relative cultural distance between home and host countries. Using available data-banks and running various statistical tests, Kogut and Singh concluded that when economic choice, in this case modes of entry, is compared across countries, cultural characteristics are likely to have profound implications.

However, it is worth noting that the data-banks that Kogut and Singh used for their statistical analyses concerned only EU and Japanese multinational firms' investment in the United States. Moreover, the exercise provided only a statistical support for the role of the country of origin and its cultural distance in investment decisions, which does not necessarily demonstrate causal linkages between the two sets of variables. An extensive interview programme with the relevant executives in these companies, or at least a representative sample of them, might have been more illuminating.

The fact that many western and south-east Asian multinational firms have set up business in all corners of the world, most of them culturally and psychically poles apart from their cultural origins, demonstrates the weakness of psychic/cultural distance propositions. O'Grady and Lane's (1996) study, which rejects to some extent the influence of psychic/cultural distance on internationalisation strategic decisions, provides a further empirical evidence for this point from a different angle. In their study of Canadian retailers operating in the United States, O'Grady and Lane found that although the Canadian companies in their sample began their internationalisation by entering the United States, a country culturally closest to their home country, when one looks beyond the sequence of entry to performance one encounters a paradox. Instead of similar cultures being easy to enter and to do business in, the researchers argue, it may be very difficult to enter these markets because decision-makers may not be prepared for differences.

As was discussed in Chapter 2, membership of supranational organisations and conventions could help expansion strategies of the member states' firms. It is much easier, for instance, for EU companies to move around within the member states, to merge, to takeover, to set up green-field sites, to enter into strategic alliances and joint ventures, than would otherwise be the case. The freedom of movement of people, goods, services and capital, the harmonisation of various laws, and deregulation in the business arena, have greatly facilitated such expansions. NAFTA, too, though much more limited in scope compared to the EU's arrangements, has liberated the internationalisation strategies of the companies in the three member states from unhelpful obstacles to a great extent.

FINANCIAL MATTERS

Raising funds for investment, especially in host countries, can be a complex affair for firms with operations in different nations. There could be various financial and political reasons for a company's decision to borrow money locally. Low interest rates and other favourable terms might be one such reason. Also, in some 'risk-prone' countries, a foreign firm might like to raise capital locally and thereby entwine its interests with those of the local banks, a strategy which in turn might act as a deterrent to possible hostile actions by the host government in the future. Since capital markets around the world have different structures (see also Chapter 3), companies which would like to raise capital locally need to adjust to these differences, which have their roots in some cases in their respective national ways of doing things.

In many developing countries and some of the ex-socialist economies, capital markets are either nonexistent or in the early stages of their formation and development. Moreover, in some cases banks lend money to local companies not on the basis of information about their performances, which can be sketchy, out of date and often unreliable, but on the basis of informal connections and networks (Enthoven, 1977). Financial institutions which lend money to business enterprises, instead of relying on less-than-dependable financial reports take other factors, such as the reputation of the borrower, the lender's personal knowledge about the borrower's financial creditability, and substantial security pledged in the form of personal property, into consideration when evaluating the creditworthiness of the borrowing companies. Such practices could be so firmly embedded in the national financial culture that they might not allow exceptions to be made for foreign firms with creditable documents about their performance as security for loans.

As for the profits that a foreign firm would make in host countries, some governments impose restrictions on profit repatriation, or might ask the foreign firm to plough back a certain percentage of its annual profits into the local economy, in both commercial and social projects.

PROJECT VERSUS CONTINUOUS OPERATIONS

In deciding to have international business dealings, especially in the service sector and in the manufacturing sector in case of activities such as outsourcing, companies might choose their operations on the basis of a series of projects or a continuous one, or a combination of the two. Whatever form they opt for, these firms might encounter certain culturally-rooted complications.

Within the context of the service sector, Nahapiet (1998) points out that firms handle the way they relate to their clients in a variety of ways along a continuum stretching from project management to relationship management. In traditional project management, services are planned and delivered on a discrete project-by-project basis. Projects may be large and complex and span several countries, thus involving extensive contacts with clients. Indeed, there may be a series of projects for a particular client. But there is no presumption of a continuous relationship and projects are not managed with continuity in mind. Each exchange is essentially episodic and transactional. For the client, relationship-by-project provides the benefits of flexibility, lower prices and the chance to choose the service provider best suited to each project. For the service firm, it also offers flexibility, reduces overdependence on particular clients and allows for the development of specialist skills.

By contrast, relationship management is an approach rooted in continuity, interdependence and partnership over time. It values 'share of client' at least as highly as share of market. Relationship management demands a significant investment in getting to know and understand the client and in developing a unique relationship well beyond the confines of specific projects. It is built on the assumption that partnerships are both valuable and valued, and as such constitutes a powerful differentiating force in markets where services are often viewed as commodities.

Following further from the above, one could argue that certain cultures like that of Japan, Southeast Asia and the Middle East nations, favour a relationship-oriented style in business dealings. Relationships with suppliers, clients, customers, employees and the like are nurtured, built up, and imbued with mutual trust over a long period of time, and are not easily abandoned even if they might cause temporary financial losses. Chinese family-centred networks, Arabs' informal networks rooted in their tribal heritage, and tiered relationships with suppliers and subcontractors in Japanese *keiretsu* rooted in their collectivism and community-centred traditions, are manifestations of the relationship-oriented ways of doing business. This style is obviously compatible with and encourages a continuous operations strategy.

By contrast, the contract-oriented business relationships especially favoured by Anglo-American firms, anchored in their legalistic approach to business and the individualism of their cultural heritage, favours a project operations strategy.

Dore (1997, p. 23) sums up the contrast nicely:

> British or American businesspersons are apt to think that the efficiency of their business depends on always keeping an eagle eye open for trends in the market. They should always be comparing the ideal they are getting from a particular supplier with what they could get elsewhere – and switch without compunction if they find a better combination of quality and price. The Japanese, by contrast, operate with a sense of obligation. Trading relations are seen as generating mutual obligations; as long as the supplier is fulfilling his part of the bargain, 'genuinely and sincerely doing his best' to maintain quality and delivery times, to sink capital in the relationships in order to speed up the joint development of new products, to cooperate in cost cutting when the market turns down, he has a right not to be abandoned because, perhaps for circumstances beyond his control, another supplier offers a better deal.

TECHNOLOGY TRANSFER

Technology and technology development strategies form a significant part of a company's current and future plans. Whereas cross-border transfers between nations of similar cultural and infrastructural levels might with slight adaptations be an easily managed process, such transfers to countries with a fundamentally different set of values and institutional supports than the parent company's home country could be difficult if not impossible.

Culturally, as Hofstede (1980, p. 300) points out,

> ... technologies are not neutral with regard to values; in order to work, they assume that certain values are respected. Making these technologies work means that people in the receiving countries must learn new leadership and subordinateship skills, change old institutions and shift their values. Cultural transposition, in the ideal case, means finding a new cultural synthesis which retains from the old local values those elements deemed essential but which allows the new technologies to function. Attempts at the transfer of leadership skills which do not take the values of subordinates into account have little chance of success.

In addition to certain cultural incompatibilities with technologies developed elsewhere, there are other aspects of culture which might interfere with the transfer process. The Arab nations' unease about western technologies and know-how in general, deeply rooted in their history and their relationships with certain western nations, is a case in point.

For over seven centuries Arab Muslims ruled over a large part of the world from the Atlantic coast to India. The attitudes developed in the wake of such a cultural dominance, as Solberg (1998) argues, are maybe mirrored in what western managers often experience as a sentiment of cultural superiority by the Arabs: they consider themselves to be at the top of the cultural hierarchy and regard other cultures with lenience and suspicion. There is also tension between western technology and the rational thinking behind it on the one hand, and the desire to maintain an Islamic spiritualism on the other (Brögger, 1993, cited in Solberg, 1998). Even if the Arabs may trust western technology, they often express doubts about western managers' sincerity and motives because of their experience with the west, especially during British and French rule, followed by the neo-colonialism of the United States after the Second World War (Ali, 1995). This experience, together with their perceived technological inferiority, could cause tension between Arabs and their western trading partners.

Training may help people overcome a lack of skills, and the organisational culture could help eradicate some cultural causes of suspicions and dysfunctions, but this requires sensitivity on the part of the parent company and a willingness on the part of the foreign subsidiary.

The encounter with foreign technology and ways of doing things need not always and in all countries be a negative experience, even though the recipients might be culturally distant from the foreign parent company. McDonald's experience in Moscow for instance demonstrates the wholeheartedness with which the young recruits, local managers and local suppliers embraced the company's style both in managerial and non-managerial aspects of the business (Vikhanski and Puffer, 1993). In this case the favourable working conditions and pay and other benefits, and also the pride the local people felt in working for a multinational firm of McDonald's stature and reputation in comparison with the plight of their fellow Russians, may have contributed to the positive reception of foreign ideas and technologies.

SUMMARY

In international firms, and indeed in single-nation firms, the development of various strategies, we have argued, is not independent of its socio-political context. Company goals and different ways of achieving them through, for instance, expanding abroad vary from country to country depending on their own specific circumstances. Financial matters such as raising capital, operational matters such as choosing between continuous and project businesses with foreign clients and customers, and transferring technology from home-country to foreign lands, all bring firms with international operations head to head with other people's nationally and culturally embedded ways of doing things.

In addition, there are complications which arise from certain host-country historical and deep-rooted sensibilities and sensitivities which interfere with the smooth and company-wide implementation of strategies devised in the headquarters in far away places, both literally and figuratively. In this chapter we have identified some of these issues and discussed their implications for international firms.

7 Organisational Design

INTRODUCTION

Multinational companies share in common with their single-nation counterparts many internal organisational issues, problems and challenges, such as coordination, integration, differentiation and control, but they face these in their most intense and complex forms. The sheer size and diversity of location, products and services offered and needed, operational technology, clients, suppliers, customers, legal and other institutional contacts and trade partners, bring with them their own imperatives. These in turn cause conflicts, frictions, tensions and frustrations in their own right in addition to those which might have their roots in the national culture of the parent company and its foreign subsidiaries.

Conflict can occur at a number of levels, between head office and subsidiaries (or agents, affiliates and franchisees, as may be the case), between subsidiaries and their host country, or within head office. In addition there may also be communication difficulties between head office and subsidiaries.

As Wilson and Rosenfeld (1990) argue, conflict primarily occurs over priorities in decision-making within the multinational firm. Decisions concerning organisational structure present a considerable challenge to the manager of international companies. Do managers organise on product lines or should the firm be structured on the basis of its geographical markets? Should they create a separate 'international division' at head office to handle multinational problems centrally, or should most decision-making be decentralised to the operating subsidiaries? Companies which have adopted a product structure have generally done so due to the differing technologies associated with each product. In such a structure, management power is usually rooted in its knowledge of a technologically complex product. For this reason, a central international division may cause difficulties since various product divisions tend to reserve all policy decisions pertaining to international operations for themselves. This reduces the influence of the international division's managers on overall strategies and policy decisions, and international conflict becomes inevitable.

However, market-structured organisations are also prone to the problems resulting from cross-cultural differences, as it can prove difficult to transfer policies and strategies across territorial boundaries. This can readily produce conflicts between subsidiaries and head office, inter-subsidiary conflicts, and conflict between the needs of production and markets.

Decisions over production can also present their challenges to the international manager. Foreign production capacity implies a decision to engage in international competition through the entire transformation process from raw materials to finished goods. The challenge of international production facilities, therefore, lies in the need to understand the implications of variations in the economic, social and political environments of the countries in which it produces goods as well as those where the goods are sold (Wilson and Rosenfeld, 1990).

The complexity of the structure of the international firm will have a marked effect on the ease or difficulty with which information is transmitted across the organisation. Perlmutter (1969) suggests that the key to understanding communication is to examine the relationships between head office and its international operations. The level of decentralisation, the extent to which the international organisation operates globally, and the structure of the firm will all create potential problems for communication. In extreme cases, head office can be unaware of critical information, or may misunderstand completely the information coming from subsidiaries (Robock and Simmonds, 1983). Communication in the ethnocentric perspective, for example, can suffer from both blinkered thinking and the exercise of power. Head office strategies become in danger of institutionalisation, with the preclusion of certain attitudes and behaviours. In companies with polycentric strategies communication difficulties can arise from the duplication of effort between subsidiaries and from the inefficient use of head office experience (Heenan and Perlmutter, 1979).

The following sections discuss some of the major organisational issues which cause tension and conflict within the politically, economically and culturally-diverse context of international firms.

DIFFERENTIATION AND INTEGRATION DILEMMAS

One of the preoccupations of both scholars and practitioners regarding the organisation of an international firm is the relationship between a parent company and its subsidiaries which are inherently prone to tension and conflicts, mainly because of the geographical and culturally differentiated nature of such a firm and the need to keep it as a consistent 'whole', to rationalise the use of resources, and to serve its large and complex market more effectively. People have argued extensively about the balance to be struck between the need for responsiveness to local conditions and the desire to maintain integration throughout the firm.

The concepts of differentiation and integration were borrowed from sociology and applied within the context of management and organisation studies by Lawrence and Lorsch (1967). They argued that for an organisation to perform effectively in diverse environments, it must be both appropriately differentiated and adequately integrated in order that the separate units and departments are coordinated and work towards a common goal. The differentiation that the authors had in mind had to do with the mind sets and ways of doing things that each functional part of a (single-nation) firm might develop in response to its own specific segment of environment. Lawrence and Lorsch's (1967) model has been developed further for international firms in order to explain the dynamics of managing organisations operating across borders (see for example, Doz, 1976; Prahalad, 1976; Laurent, 1986; Prahalad and Doz, 1987; Bartlett and Ghoshal, 1989; Ghoshal and Bartlett, 1992; Schuler *et al.*, 1993; Welch, 1994; Nahapiet, 1998).

Obviously, the significance and relevance of the question of integration and differentiation varies from firm to firm depending on their degrees of internationalisation. The deeper and wider a firm is internationalised the more complicated and bigger its problem of differentiation and integration becomes. For a firm which internationalises by buying up share portfolios in firms operating abroad, the differentiation and integration dilemma does not exist at all. For an exporting firm, it is the marketing function, and to some extent the product specifications, which need to be rearranged to enable the firm to respond to its differentiated customer base. For a firm which franchises or licenses out the manufacture and delivery of its products and services to local operators, negotiation and partner relations skills would need to be differentiated more than most functions to take local culture and traditions into account.

For a company which invests abroad and becomes involved in locally-based operations, in the form of joint ventures and wholly-owned subsidiaries, either as a 'global' business or a multi-domestic one, the issue of integration and differentiation will be at its most acute. The appropriate mix of differentiation and integration depends on many factors, some of which will be discussed below, and is often difficult to achieve successfully.

On the parent company's side, the degree to which freedom of action is granted to subsidiaries depends on the parent company's overall strategy based in part on its fundamental philosophy, values and beliefs as well as on business imperatives. From a cultural perspective it is reasonable to assume that companies which start off their lives, perhaps as family-owned entities, in a country where the prevalent value systems encourage respect for other peoples' viewpoints, egalitarian relationships between the partners involved in a social transaction, and, in short, democratic power relationships, such value systems might be reflected in those companies' management styles and organisational structures.

By contrast, if the home country's culture is characterised by non-egalitarian power relationships, a concentration of power and control in the hands of a few 'wise and privileged' people, based perhaps on their wealth and political influence, such characteristics might also prevail in their multinational companies.

The influence of home-based ways of doing things on those of foreign subsidiaries may vary depending also on whether or not the parent company managers believe their ways are superior to those of the host countries. The parent's superiority in technological and managerial know-how over its subsidiaries places it in a powerful position, especially in those cases where subsidiaries are located in less economically advanced nations compared to the home country. But if a parent company invests in a host nation with the specific intention of tapping the local managerial know-how and technical skills it is likely that the subsidiary will have more autonomy and power than would otherwise be the case.

Moreover, whereas parent companies may be willing to decentralise operative and other non-strategic decisions, they might, as Poynter and Rugman (1982) and Crookell (1986) argue, be reluctant to cede the control of strategically important activities to subsidiaries. Most multinational companies used to be, and many still are, reluctant to locate their R&D activities in their foreign subsidiaries. The reason may not entirely be on the ground of a lack of expertise in host nations, as evidenced by many Japanese and American firms which do not take their R&D functions to the countries with equal if not better records in scientific research and innovation, and with skilled workforces. R&D functions represent the heart and brains of a company, as it were, as are strategic industries for nations – one does not want such a source of life and power to go to foreigners.

A related point to note is that some researchers argue that the autonomy, the so-called mandate, that a subsidiary might enjoy (Roth and Morrison, 1992; Moore, 1994; Birkinshaw, 1995) is not given by the parent company but earned by the subsidiary. However, there is a danger of multinational firms losing their best local employees if they are denied autonomy and the chance of progressing up the real decision-making hierarchy (see for instance Rosenzweig, 1994). Also, the extent to which the parent company can control or influence relevant events and issues especially in the host country will have a great impact upon its power to dominate the parent–subsidiary relationship. Here is where the subsidiary's potential, if not actual, power and influence come into play.

Local managers, especially in some nations in Southeast Asia and the Middle East, where informal connections and personal networks greatly enhance the chances of success and getting things done, will have the upper hand *vis-à-vis* their HQ managers hundreds of miles away, socio-culturally as well as geographically. The familiarity with local conditions goes, of course, beyond informal relations. Knowing one's own country's legal systems, being in touch with political events, being aware of the latest changes in laws, rules and regulations, and keeping abreast of the latest developments in fads and fashions and customers' tastes, are also contributory factors to the balance of power within the parent–subsidiary relationship.

It has been argued that the extent of autonomy granted to a subsidiary by its parent company could in part depend on the strength of the former's entrepreneurial culture (Kuratko *et al.*, 1990), where risk-taking and entrepreneurial activities are promoted (Birkinshaw and Hood, 1998). The social anthropology literature and cross-cultural studies of work-related values show that entrepreneurial culture is not present with equal intensity around the world, and, moreover, it can diminish or increase over time. A comparative study of the UK and the USA by Wiener (1981) showed that Americans are far more entrepreneurial than their British counterparts. Moreover, the Britons of the eighteenth and nineteenth centuries appear to have been endowed with a higher degree of entrepreneurial spirit than their twentieth century descendants (Barnett, 1972; Roderick and Stephenson, 1978, 1981, 1982).

Risk-taking, too, seems to have some cultural roots. Risk-taking presupposes tolerance for ambiguity and uncertainty, and the 40 nations that Hofstede (1980) included in his study displayed a remarkable degree of variation on this trait.

In the light of these cultural differences and variations, one would imagine that foreign subsidiaries of a multinational firms will have different degrees of autonomy as to how they run their affairs, depending in part on their culturally-rooted ability to take risks and engage in entrepreneurial activities. In addition to cultural capabilities, the standing of a subsidiary in the local economy, its age and experience in the business and the in-house expertise and competence could place it in a powerful position in relation to its parent company.

In a case study (Tayeb 1998) the present author found that the Scottish subsidiary of an American firm enjoyed a certain amount of autonomy and freedom in the way in which its internal affairs were being organised and managed. Moreover, the subsidiary had 'earned' two further 'privileges' normally denied to many subsidiaries of the same firm elsewhere. In most cases, foreign subsidiaries were for many years managed at senior levels by expatriates from the HQ, with the exception, perhaps, of personnel or human-resources functions. But here in Scotland the situation was different. The MD was a Scotsman, and was the first chief executive officer of the company who was a non-American. At the time of the study, with a few exceptions, other directors and senior managers were all local. This subsidiary later on set a trend for employment of local personnel in senior positions in many of the firm's foreign subsidiaries.

The second significant privilege was that the Scottish subsidiary housed and managed an R&D department with 300 professionals and a highly skilled technical staff who were engaged in innovative activities and served the whole of the company worldwide in one of its main product lines. This had been achieved after years of experimentation leading to accumulation of valuable expertise, and also the local managers' ability to identify and exploit the opportunities which presented themselves.

There were also two further factors which had contributed to all this. The managing director had been hired in the early 1980s to save an ailing subsidiary or else close it down. In a way, the parent company had nothing to lose by giving the MD the freedom that he wanted. Also, the subsidiary had been in place for over fifty years and had developed its own ways of doing things, which proved most of the time to be appropriate for its business and location. The company enjoys a strong organisational culture which has evolved over a period of half a century. In particular, after the change of leadership in the early 1980s, managers and employees alike underwent an extraordinary shared experience of turning an ailing company into a hugely successful world-class organisation. They had all made great sacrifices to achieve this and were proud of it. Interwoven in this organisational culture was a leadership which glued the various parts of the subsidiary into a coherent entity. This entity, although it was capable of absorbing change and accommodating new ways of doing things, resisted overt imposition and interference from outside, be it a management fad or a directive from on high.

However, the subsidiary is well-integrated into the larger holding company, and its strategies are those of the parent company's to a large extent. What takes place in Scotland is in no way detrimental to the overall interests of the company as a whole, but is a successful example of a balance between differentiation and integration sought after by so many multinational firms with subsidiaries around the world. But, some of the parent company's strategies and policies have been interpreted in a locally acceptable manner and translated into practices which work better hundreds of miles away from where they were originated. This local interpretation has in fact been one of the major reasons why differentiation and integration processes have gone hand in hand successfully in the firm.

An aspect of a foreign subsidiary's experience which could earn it autonomy is related directly to their local business environment. Building on Porter's (1990) model, Birkinshaw and Hood (1998) argue that one of the factors which would contribute to the presence of subsidiary mandate is local market competitiveness, demanding customers and strong supporting and related industries in the local business environment. Such an environment, as is for instance the case in Japan and many similar advanced capitalist nations, helps local managers gain invaluable experience and training, which in turn places them in an advantageous position. But of course many countries lack such vibrant domestic environments for historical, cultural and political reasons, as has been discussed in earlier chapters. As a result, subsidiaries of foreign firms located in such countries will not have the same earned mandates as their, say, Japanese or American counterparts.

In addition, unfavourable local economic conditions such as recessions and high rates of unemployment can adversely affect the subsidiaries' power and influence, regardless of their excellent locally-acquired experience. In such cases the parent company can dictate terms, both in strategic spheres and with respect to operative decisions such as quality control, arrangements with local suppliers and management–subordinate relationships (Tayeb, 1994; Beechler and Yang, 1994).

It is worth noting that the push towards integration comes not only from within the firm, but also, indirectly at least, from the outside interests, such as clients and suppliers. As clients integrate their activities across borders they often look to their service providers to do the same, and as companies globalise, they generally seek suppliers who can cater for them as a single entity and provide them with a consistent and coordinated cross-border service. Moves to regional and global branding, for example, require corresponding support teams at regional and

global levels – both in the client company and the supporting advertising agency. Similarly, the growing regional or global concentration of
specialist functions in areas such as research and development and
manufacturing often calls for regional or global consulting teams
(Nahapiet, 1998).

The distinction between culture-specific and universal aspects of
management may also be relevant to the debate regarding the management of foreign subsidiaries in particular, and the question of differentiation and integration in general. Tayeb's (1988) study of a sample of
English and Indian manufacturing firms demonstrated that both cultural and non-cultural factors play a part in the management of an
organisation, with soft culture-specific aspects looking different across
nations, and hard culture-free aspects appearing similar regardless of
location.

A recent case study in three American subsidiaries and affiliates
located in Scotland (Tayeb and Dott, 2000) revealed an interesting pattern which supports this line of argument. The study found that the
so-called 'soft' aspects of management, such as interpersonal relationships and communication, HRM and industrial relations issues, were
influenced by the local culture and handled according to locally accepted
norms and traditions, even though in some cases the parent company
was unhappy with the outcome. On the other hand, certain culture-free
and so-called 'hard' aspects of management such as strategy, budgetary
control, hierarchical structure and the use of standard procedures and
rules, were decided by the parent companies and implemented more or
less unchallenged and unchanged in the Scottish plants.

The study showed that the American multinational companies' preferred way of organising and controlling their subsidiaries in Scotland
was to delegate as much autonomy as possible to the local management
in charge, but at the same time this decentralisation was accompanied
by detailed written policies, rules and regulations. This is not dissimilar
to the policies and practices employed by most large-scale organisations, multinational or otherwise, with a wide range of functions and
operations. In other words, the three multinational companies involved
in the study had differentiated those aspects of their subsidiaries' management which were closely affected by local sociocultural conditions,
but had maintained the integration of the company as a whole by centrally controlling those organisational aspects which were relatively
culture-neutral.

To sum up this section, parent–subsidiary relationships, and the consequent balance between differentiation and integration, represent a

dynamic, fluid and continuously-changing state, often resolved on a one-to-one basis (Tayeb, 1998). This view is in line with Ghoshal and Bartlett's arguments (1990) and contrasts with the view held by some researchers (for example Hulbert and Brandt, 1980) who see multinational firms as homogeneous entities, especially with regard to parent–subsidiary relationships.

INTERNATIONAL ENTERPRISES AS DIFFERENTIATED NETWORKS

The use of the concept of networking has recently been suggested as a means of examining how global businesses relate to their subsidiaries and other internal units as well as the outside world (Ghoshal and Bartlett, 1990; Forsgren and Johanson, 1992). Networking, as we shall see below, is increasingly replacing the traditional hierarchical structure as a means of maintaining integration while remaining responsive to local conditions.

Ghoshal and Bartlett (1990) compare the multinational company to a network of relationships between and among parent and subsidiaries. In addition, each subsidiary as well as the HQ are embedded in their own respective local networks of organisations and institutions with which they develop their own linkages and relationships. Given the cultural political and legal diversity of the nations within which various units of a multinational firm are situated, the network density within each host country and as a result across the firm varies from location to location.

Further, they argue that the allocation of a firm's resources, such as production equipment, finance, technology, marketing skills and management capabilities, to various subsidiaries depends on a number of criteria, including their local networking density. For instance, in some locations internal interactions within the local organisation sets may be high, but external linkages within other organisation sets may be low. In such locations, the multinational firm may provide all the required resources in appropriate measures so that its local subsidiary can build and maintain linkages with key members of its own community. By comparison, the organisation sets in some other countries may be sparsely connected internally, but different elements of the local environment may be strongly connected with their counterparts in other countries. For such locations, the company may create a resource structure that is concentrated and specialised. In some cases the location of the specialised resource may reflect the desire to access special resource niches, but in other cases the location choice may be motivated by modalities of the external network.

MECHANISMS TO ACHIEVE INTEGRATION

Many traditional devices such as budgetary control, formalised rules and regulations, performance criteria and intra-firm accounting practices can be put in place to make subsidiaries work towards a common goal and to coordinate their activities. Expatriate managers dispatched from the HQ to control and/or train local managers are another traditional channel to create and maintain integration.

However, increasingly, companies are attempting to address the tensions caused by the concern for differentiation and integration from a novel perspective. Rather than trying to balance the contradictions by, for example, trading some degree of integration for some degree of responsiveness, the best global competitors are instead attempting to maximise both these dimensions. This approach, as Pucik (1998) points out, represents a shift away from structural solutions to the challenges of global business organisation. It replaces the continuous oscillation between centralisation and decentralisation with an acceptance of the global organisation as a fluid and dynamic network. Networking focuses on the management process, not on organisational structure and procedures.

Relationship management, which is at the heart of networking among various units of a multinational firm, provides among other things consistency and coherence through the establishment of strong and integrated relationships within the company regardless of specific geographical locations. It fosters integration and coordination and creates and supports a sense of common purpose, trust and cooperation among all units. Relationship management is an approach rooted in continuity, interdependence and partnership over time and demands a significant investment in getting to know and understand one another. It seeks to establish strong and integrated relationships with individuals on a company-wide basis (Nahapiet, 1998).

A major objective of such networks of relationships is to spread around value systems to which the firm would wish to subscribe and which form the basis of its organisational culture. However, the extent to which values could be shared throughout the firm is not certain. (see for instance Ghoshal's (1986) attempt at establishing the extent of normative integration in a sample of companies). Moreover, as we shall see in a later chapter, organisational culture as a form of normative integration mechanism may be unable to eradicate people's culturally-rooted values and attitudes, it may only encourage them to subscribe to certain expected practices (Hofstede *et al.*, 1990).

In any case, creating such inter-unit networks across nations is not easy. The individuals and units involved have to face not only different national cultures, with different perceptions of power, approaches to efficiency, methods of cooperation and so on, but also an unfamiliar professional culture, as an example given by Chassang and Reitter (1998) demonstrates. In one international manufacturing firm the German and Spanish units complained about the UK 'procurement' culture. The relationship between some UK units and their internal suppliers was managed not by the project managers in charge of the final assembly, but by a procurement department that also dealt with external suppliers. The internal suppliers were treated in the same formal, contractual and at times aggressive manner as external ones. What is more, each unit was required to supply components according to convenient splits in the equipment to be produced but with no regard to the technical interfacing between elements. The procurement officers had no technical expertise and therefore adopted a purely purchasing-oriented approach more appropriate for standard components that can easily be integrated into a final product. There was no attempt to act together to anticipate and solve common problems. This gave rise to disputes over changes and delays as technical interfacing became an issue later in the assembly process.

As Nahapiet (1998) points out, a different mindset is needed to participate in global relationship management, the key features of which are realistic expectations, a cosmopolitan and collaborative outlook, high levels of trust and a willingness to learn from one another.

Also, some multinational firms might develop a structure which Bartlett and Ghoshal (1989) describe as a *differentiated network*, and which is suggested with regard to resource configuration (Ghoshal and Bartlett, 1990). But one can just as easily apply it within the context of attempts to create shared values. That is, value systems created in certain parts of the company, say among the subsidiaries located in Anglo-Saxon regions, may reflect the region's historical and cultural heritage, whereas those created in the Arab Middle East and other Muslim nations may be coloured by their Islamic heritage.

This now brings the discussion to the organisational design and structure at the local, subsidiary level.

A SUBSIDIARY'S ORGANISATIONAL STRUCTURE AND MANAGEMENT STYLE

Responsiveness and differentiation mean, of course, allocating resources and responsibilities to subsidiaries depending on their local conditions and letting them get on with it. It must also mean allowing subsidiaries to organise their internal affairs and decide on their own management styles. Here the role of national culture is obviously significant.

Decision-making processes, including power and authority relationships, risk-taking, and ensuring the implementation of decisions, are fertile grounds for people's cultural values and attitudes to manifest themselves and to influence the course of events. In some nations, people are brought up to be deferential or even obedient to those in positions of power, who in turn expect obedience and deference from subordinates. In other nations power relationships between such actors is less inegalitarian and both junior and senior partners may exert power and influence over one another. Similarly, nations differ from one another in respect of ability to cope with uncertainty and risk, attitudes to control and motivation and preferred mechanisms for control and motivation. These culturally-rooted characteristics are by implication out of the reach and power of a parent company's managers who are situated in a faraway place, both geographically and culturally.

Moreover, organisational structure is more than just the formal manifestation of its hierarchical order and rules and procedures. The parallel, sometimes more potent, informal relationships among employees and between subordinates and superiors can in fact be the real arena where the organisational drama is played out. Here the influence of the parent company is further diminished, as such informal relationships cannot be regulated, supervised, controlled and shaped from a distance.

In addition to local cultural characteristics, contextual variables such as size, industry, technology, status and ownership play a significant role in shaping decision-making structures and management styles – the so-called contingency model. For example, an increase in the number of employees leads to an increase in the specialisation of functions, the formalisation of rules and regulations, and the decentralisation of decision-making. The same is the case with old organisations in comparison with younger ones, and so on. In relation to multinational firms, although some of the contextual factors could be similar across subsidiaries, especially in those firms which produce one main product or use one main technology, some factors such as size may still be different from subsidiary to subsidiary. In highly diversified global companies, almost all the contextual variables could be different in different subsidiaries.

As a result, one might observe specific organisational structures and arrangements in a subsidiary that are compatible with its own respective contextual factors, which might vary from those of other subsidiaries of the same holding company but located elsewhere on the globe facing different contexts.

In addition, although subsidiaries in some nations can organise themselves 'freely' in response to their contextual factors, and move between various forms of structures (Burns and Stalker, 1961), in some nations the national culture might set limits as to how far they go along these lines (Tayeb, 1979, 1995). In other words, in some countries local as well as foreign firms may be able to adopt a democratic decentralised model because the local national culture supports such models, but in some other nations the workable model might be a centralised one because the existing political, cultural and educational infrastructure does not support any other.

SUMMARY

This chapter has mainly discussed the question of differentiation and integration, one of the major issues confronting firms with international business, especially those with foreign affiliates and subsidiaries in which local people are employed. It has been argued, along with many scholars and writers in the field, that while it is imperative for such firms to maintain their integrity and 'wholeness' in terms of overall direction and strategic thrust, it is very difficult if not impossible to remain indifferent to local variations in customer base, clients, employees, suppliers and other contacts. These local variations are, of course, rooted in age-old national cultures and other socio-political and economic institutions and policies, some of which may result in practices and policy preferences totally in opposition to what the parent company might have in mind.

It is stressed, however, that the issue of differentiation and integration should not be conceived of as a choice between the two options or a balance between them; rather, they may indeed be complementary to one another and one might achieve differentiation without it being at the expense of integration.

It seems, on the whole, that the culture-specific aspects of international firms such as leadership and human-resource management style, negotiation, advertising and relationships with suppliers, in short parts of the operation which bring people and their values and attitudes into contact with one another, tend to be differentiated in response to local conditions. But universal, culture-free aspects of firms, such as divisional-isation of operations, budgetary control, financial targets to be achieved by senior managers and related periodical progress reports and the like, are ripe for maximum integration and harmonisation across all the units, affiliates and subsidiaries (see also Tayeb and Dott, 2000).

8 Human Resource Management

INTRODUCTION

Human resource management (HRM) has been defined in many ways and various models have been developed and discussed to tease out its specific character (see for example Legge (1995) for a thorough review and analysis of the literature). HRM is clearly rooted in its ancestor, personnel management, with a strategic slant (Legge 1989; Poole, 1990; Storey, 1992; Schuler *et al.*, 1993). So, in fact, one still deals with issues such as selection, recruitment, training, remuneration and the like, the preserve of personnel management. But all these issues are considered bearing the overall strategies of the firm in mind and the ways in which HRM can contribute to those strategies.

In addition, HRM has been viewed from two different but not necessarily incompatible perspectives (Legge, 1995): hard and soft (Storey, 1987; Hendry and Pettigrew, 1990). According to the hard model, reflecting utilitarian instrumentalism, HRM is used to drive the strategic objectives of the firm (Fomburn *et al.*, 1984) and that human resource, the object of formal manpower planning, is a 'resource', like other factors of production, and an expense of doing business rather than the only resource capable of turning inanimate factors of production into wealth (Tyson and Fell, 1986).

Some might argue that this is a degrading view of humans and in any case ignores fundamental differences between people and other resources. Production factors other than humans are comparatively less anchored and therefore can be moved around, shuffled, reduced, increased, transformed and discarded relatively freely to suit managers' requirements. Their value is subject to market forces in most cases in a straightforward manner. But humans are different. They have needs, emotions, interests and attachments, and they perform their tasks best if these are reasonably catered for. They cannot be easily discarded and shuffled around against their wishes without causing individual and/or social upset. A woman manager with young children and a working husband and located in London, is far less mobile compared to a sum of £200 000 which can be electronically transferred from the City of London to Hong Kong within seconds (Tayeb, 1996a).

Concerns such as these are encapsulated in what is called a soft, developmental humanism view of HRM. This model, while still emphasising the importance of integrating human resource policies with business objectives, sees this as involving treating employees as valued assets, a source of competitive advantage through their commitment, adaptability and high quality (Storey, 1987; Vaughan, 1994). According to this view, employees are proactive inputs in production processes and are capable of development, worthy of trust and collaboration, to be achieved through participation and informed choice. The stress is therefore on generating commitment via communication, motivation and leadership. If employees' commitment yields better economic performance, it is also sought as a route to greater human development (Beer and Spector, 1985; Walton, 1985; Storey, 1987).

Human resources, however viewed, must function and be managed in such a manner as to support the rapid pace of internationalisation of companies and enhance and maintain their competitiveness in the marketplace. As Pucik (1998) points out, many companies competing globally are facing a multitude of new demands on their organisational structures and personnel. Often they are pushed simultaneously in several contradictory strategic directions. In order to survive and prosper in the global competitive environment, companies are embracing closer regional and global integration and coordination. At the same time, they face demands for local responsiveness, flexibility and speed. Human resources are very much part and parcel of all this.

This chapter focuses on major issues which multinational firms face in setting out and implementing their HRM strategies across their multicultural organisations.

NATIONAL CULTURE AND THE HRM CONCEPT

The definition and major models of HRM, as outlined above, have certain underlying assumptions which are by their nature highly culture-specific. Needless to say, the models and the concept of HRM itself are a product of Anglo-American scholarly culture rooted in their own wider societal cultures, which are not of course either universally valued or appreciated as relevant.

Clark and Pugh (1998), building on the vast literature on the implications of national culture for management techniques and models, conducted a 'polycentric' study into the conceptions of HRM, a US-grown concept, in a sample of European countries, namely Germany, the UK,

Denmark, Spain, France, Sweden and the Netherlands. The authors found that the concept of HRM has not been accepted or established as an academic discipline evenly among the sampled nations. For instance, there has been little discussion of HRM in Spain, due to a period of shake-out of labour, with rising redundancies and unemployment, which the country has been undergoing for some time now. This has meant that appreciation of the competitive value of human resources which is at the basis of HRM has not been much in evidence. In Denmark, the Netherlands and Sweden, HRM is subsumed in other social science discipline areas and has yet to emerge as a distinctive academic subject. It is only in Britain and Germany that HRM has developed into a distinctive and fully-fledged academic area with all the accompanying professional activities.

The authors further found that a large number of the sampled nations agreed on three elements of HRM: the importance of human resources as a source of competitive advantage, the decentralisation of responsibility for HR issues to the firm and/or line management, and the integration of HR strategies with corporate strategies to make them mutually reinforcing. However, there were differences with regard to the importance of these elements and also their interpretations between the sampled nations. Thus, the authors argue, Sweden's strong collectivist culture counters the development of a more individualistic orientation to employment relationships, and the Dutch 'feminine' culture encourages the antipathy of Dutch employees to 'hard' HRM. Similarly, the institutional factors in Germany of the strong role of the unions and the formal consultative structures between employers and employees attenuate the rise of the managerial prerogative. In France the power of the *patronat* hinders decentralisation.

Clark and Pugh's study demonstrates that the concept of HRM, let alone its implementation, does not travel without at least a certain amount of local interpretation and modification. One could argue further that the more culturally distanced a country is from the HRM's home-country, the more difficult it will be for HRM to settle there in its purest form. Moreover, other societal institutions and characteristics, such as trade unions, the legal system, government policies and the general pattern of ownership and size of companies, could also exert influences on HRM strategies and their implementation.

For instance, in small owner-managed firms which characterise the industrial scene in large sections of the Chinese-speaking economies, and indeed many developing ones as well, it is hard to imagine a formal concept such as HRM, more suitable for large elaborate organisations, to take root. Marlow and Patten's (1993) study, conducted in a sample of small enterprises in a western nation, found no indication that strategic employee management was being employed with the intent of gaining competitive advantage. They found few owners indulged in forward planning in terms of employment. The researchers' tentative conclusion was that although there is some evidence that HRM strategies and techniques are accessible to small firms and some elements are being incorporated into the management of the employment relationship, it is doubtful if this is HRM or a new variant of informal unskilled management.

NATIONAL CULTURE AND HRM STRATEGIES

The first instinct of a multinational company might be to manage human resources as well as other resources and functions of its foreign subsidiaries according to its home-base models and ways of doing things, because they are 'logical', work well and are familiar. Moreover, some international companies, especially those from more advanced countries, often resist adapting to cultural differences because they believe their own ways of doing things is superior to those of others. The logic of local practices, in many cases tried and tested over centuries, is sometimes lost to a parent company from a different national background.

In practice, however, the complex and diverse world in which the subsidiaries are located imposes its own imperatives which cannot be ignored. Here, of course, the issue of differentiation and integration, as discussed in the previous chapter, is of the utmost relevance.

The question of how foreign subsidiaries manage their human resources could be approached from at least three angles. First, there are the parent company's overall HRM strategies. Following Perlmutter's (1969) model, multinational firms have three broad subsidiary management options at their disposal: they can choose to implement similar HRM policies and practices to those customary in the home country and ignore local conditions entirely (an ethnocentric policy); they can largely follow the practices prevalent in individual host countries (a polycentric policy); or they can devise and implement a universal companywide policy, fostered through its organisational culture and philosophy (a global policy).

Specific characteristics in the countries in which subsidiaries are located, however, might interfere with a straightforward choice of options and force multinationals to opt for a 'hybrid' strategy. In one study of manufacturing and service subsidiaries of Japanese multinational companies, for example, differences were found in the degree and nature of home-grown practices that these companies introduced into their US subsidiaries (Beechler and Yang, 1994). Another factor which might complicate HRM policy choices is the manner in which subsidiaries are set up. It is easier to impose home-grown policies on a greenfield subsidiary than on one which has joined the parent company through acquisition or merger (Tayeb, 1994).

A relevant point to make here is that there is a qualitative distinction between HRM *policies* and HRM *practices* (Schuler *et al.*, 1993). Whereas multinational firms might find it feasible to have company-wide philosophies and policies of a global or ethnocentric nature, they might find it necessary to be responsive to local conditions when it comes to HRM practices and adopt a polycentric style. The guiding principle in such cases is to keep the company as a whole intact and integrated, while at the same time allowing for a measure of differentiation when needed or desirable (Prahalad and Doz, 1987; Welch, 1994).

There is also the question of the crosscultural transfer of HRM policies and practices. Whatever HRM strategies multinational firms adopt, they are bound to confront culturally-rooted 'gaps' which are likely to exist between the policies perceived, from a distance, as desirable by home-country managers and what host-country managers are able to implement successfully. This question has for three decades or so been the central point of a lively debate among academics, and a focus of interest among managers. Some authors have emphasised the universality of organisations and similarities between them (for example, Kerr *et al.*, 1952; Cole, 1973; Hickson *et al.*, 1974; Form, 1979; Negandhi, 1979, 1985), and some others the cultural uniqueness of organisations (for example, Crozier, 1964; Meyer and Rowan, 1977; Hofstede, 1980; Lincoln *et al.*, 1981; Laurent, 1983). There are those who argue that technology carries its own imperatives: for an assembly-line automobile technology to be utilised properly a certain organisational design and management style must be adopted. An electronics company, on the other hand, would find a different design more appropriate; and so on.

As Tayeb (1988) has argued, however, the various sides of the debate are not mutually exclusive. Rather, they complement one another. That is, certain aspects of organisations are more likely to be universal, such as shopfloor layout (influenced in part by technological requirements), hierarchical structure and division of functions, whereas some areas are more culture-specific, such as human resource management (see also Chapter 7). Moreover, the fact is that organisations and their employees do not live in a vacuum, separated from their societal surroundings. National culture, as a set of values, attitudes and behaviours, includes elements which are relevant to work and organisation. These are carried into the workplace as part of the employees' cultural baggage. Work-related values and attitudes, such as power-distance, tolerance for ambiguity, honesty, pursuance of group or individual goals, work ethic and entrepreneurial spirit, form part of the cultural identity of a nation (Hofstede, 1980; Tayeb, 1988), and although employees may be required to perform certain *practices* at work, they cannot be deprived of their *values* (Hofstede *et al.*, 1990).

NATIONAL CULTURE AND HRM PRACTICES

Recruitment

The procedures that are followed by companies in various nations, be it a domestic single-nation firm or a multinational multicultural one, are different due to external as well as internal factors. In some countries, perhaps because of the advanced level of professionalisation of management, formal procedures such as assessment centres, interviews and written tests are employed to select the appropriate person. Among these nations, however, there may be subtle cultural interventions. For example, in Japan companies aim at selecting someone with broad educational qualifications who will then be put through months if not years of formal training and on-the-job cross-functional experience. The aim is to create a flexile and skilled internal workforce which would then be able to perform nearly any job if called upon.

In the USA, the selection criteria are primarily based on the specialism which would allow the new recruit to fit the already determined position, with or without further training as may seem necessary at a later stage. In response to such policies American educational establishments such as business schools, which have close relationships with major companies, are also geared to providing specialist managers and employees. They do in fact, arguably, provide training rather education for future managers.

In Britain, where such close relationships between industry and academia do not exist to any great extent, new recruits having been selected on a broadly fit-the-job basis, are then trained to perform that job properly. However, in recent years some British companies have introduced flexible working practices, especially on their shopfloors, whereby employees are expected to perform multiple functions after relevant in-house or contracted-out training.

In many traditional societies such as some Arab and non-Arab Middle East nations, recruitment especially to higher ranks is largely done through informal networks of relatives, friends and acquaintances. This should not be confused with nepotism, which of course exists in many societies industrially advanced or not. Rather, this is a time-honoured way of doing things, and is also in response to the limited scope and development of mass communication media and their use for advertising job vacancies. Moreover, many companies in some of these nations do not have highly specialised departments or functions regarding, for instance, selection and training of new recruits. Some of the western-style selection techniques have not crossed their borders yet, for better or for worse.

Multinational companies operating in various countries have the option of following the local practice or their own preferred system or a hybrid version. In any case, certain adaptation to local conditions might still be necessary to make the system workable (see for instance Tayeb (1998) regarding an American multinational in Scotland). This does not mean of course taking on board the local practices which may be dysfunctional. McDonald's joint venture in Russia (Vikhanski and Puffer, 1993) provides an example here, where certain local practices which in McDonald's views were undesirable had to be ironed out.

The company based its recruitment on a broad solicitation of applications and a competition. This was in marked contrast to the hiring practices of other foreign joint ventures which consisted of one of two practices: either hiring personnel already employed by the Russian partner, or hiring people based on patronage and influence and personal contacts. These latter practices did not guarantee the best workers. Also, workers from the Russian partner were often either unable or unwilling to work according to international standards. Not only did they need to be trained with respect to job-related skills, but their work attitudes also needed to be changed. So, the company, following their overall global strategy, placed a single advertisement in Moscow newspapers soliciting applications, which created a base for selecting the most energetic, motivated, intelligent and outgoing young men and women. McDonald's then decided to hire Moscow teenagers as crew members. Whereas the motivation for hiring teenagers in the USA is largely for economic reasons (crew members initially earn only slightly above the minimum wage), in Russia the primary reason was to hire people with no prior work experience. The idea was that it would be easier to instil McDonald's work habits and standards in people who know no other work than to disabuse people of unacceptable work habits they had acquired in previous jobs

The idea of recruiting young, inexperienced, 'uncontaminated' people and then train them, is a policy that many Japanese companies operating in the UK have also employed in the past three decades or so. Their objective has been mainly to avoid industrial relations problems, especially in the 1970s and early 1980s when UK trade unions were powerful, and strikes and other forms of industrial dispute used to disrupt the normal functioning of many firms.

Training

Training policies and practices in many countries are recognised as management's prerogative, and therefore are not prescribed by law. However, in some nations, such as France, companies larger than a certain size are required by law to spend a certain percentage of their annual turnover on employee training. In addition, as was mentioned in earlier chapters, traditionally Japanese, German and US companies spend a large amount of their time and finances on training their employees upon recruitment and also later throughout their careers with them. By comparison, some nations like the UK do not rank as high on this aspect of HRM.

In some developing countries training might take a more informal form such as learning on the job from superiors or more experienced colleagues or foreign experts who are invited from time to time to work there. For instance, Saudi Arabia hires many foreign experts in various capacities, who then familiarise local employees and managers with other ways of conducting business and performing functions, thereby providing an indirect training service. Countries which have been shunned by multinationals and foreign experts for various political and non-political reasons miss out on this source of training.

In addition, given the skill levels that some multinational firms require for the smooth running of their businesses and given the unevenness of the spread of such skills in various parts of the world, companies might have to devise vigorous training policies in some of their subsidiaries to bring them up to scratch, so to speak. In the central and eastern European nations which have, magnet-like, attracted many foreign 'capitalist' firms, training local employees has been an essential part of these firms' HRM policies. And these policies and their implementation tend to be a great deal more complicated than if the host country were a capitalist one. This is because in capitalist countries companies generally perform *similar functions* but in *different ways*. But in ex-socialist countries formerly under the communist rule, companies did not perform certain functions at all. In other words, the difference between capitalist and socialist countries is not only that of *style* but also of *substance*. For instance, an average manufacturing company in any capitalist country will have functions such as marketing, research and development, accounting, personnel/HRM, as a matter of course, and their employees are normally trained how to perform these functions. In the ex-socialist countries many of these functions were either out of the company's control or were not performed at all.

Job expectations and motivation policies

Many theories on motivation and need-hierarchies which were developed in the 1960s and 1970s had a built-in cultural bias in that they carried within them their proposers' largely Anglo-Saxon and taken-for-granted assumptions. Various crosscultural studies conducted since then have rejected the applicability of these theories in non-Anglo-Saxon nations (for example Kanuango and Mendonca, 1994). However, there are still some scholars who would argue that, following these theories, lower, extrinsic needs (such as hunger) are more active than higher intrinsic ones (such as self-actualisation) in people from less-economically-developed nations, and the reverse is the case for people from rich countries. This stance is implicit in current theories regarding inter-country differences in ethics in relation to economic development. Ethical codes are said to have been less developed in the countries which are not economically advanced (see for instance Laczniak and Murphy (1993) and their precursors, Thorelli (1981) and Thorelli and Sentell (1982). The frequent news stories about corruption and other unethical behaviours both in private and public-sector businesses and among politicians and government officials in many industrialised and rich nations demonstrate that such behaviours are not the preserve of any particular country or segment of the world. As for motivation theories, research in countries other than Anglo-Saxon nations, especially the developing ones such as India and Iran, does not support the assumptions which underlie them.

As part of an extensive multi-staged investigation into the implications of national culture for organisations, Tayeb (1988) conducted an employee-attitude survey questionnaire in a sample of English and Indian organisations. The questionnaire included, amongst others, a number of items derived from the need hierarchy and motivation theories developed by Maslow (1954) and his followers. She found that the two features which were of most importance to English employees were 'being creative and imaginative at work' and 'having an opportunity to learn new things'. These were closely followed by 'good pay' and 'job security'. 'Having freedom and independence' ranked fourth. The least important feature of the job was 'belonging to a group'.

To the Indian respondents the most important feature of a job was 'having an opportunity to learn new things'. It was followed by 'being creative and imaginative at work', 'having freedom and independence', and 'status and prestige'. 'Belonging to a group' was of least importance to the Indian employees, but they gave it significantly greater importance than did their English counterparts. In addition, freedom and independence were more important to Indian than to English employees. Good pay and fringe benefits were more important to the English than to the Indian employees.

As one can see, contrary to Anglo-Saxon theories, to Indian employees the so-called intrinsic aspects of a job – learning new things, having freedom and independence, and status and prestige – were of more importance than the so-called extrinsic ones; to the English employees a mixture of both – learning new things, being creative, good pay, job security, and having freedom and independence – was important. The author also found similar results in terms of need hierarchy and job expectations among Iranian employees in an earlier research project (Tayeb, 1979).

A more specific debate about motivation concerns the so-called need for achievement or achievement motive. In all societies the majority of people want to do well and have certain goals that they strive to achieve. McClelland (1961) argued that people's need for achievement in industrialised societies tends to be higher compared to the less economically advanced nations. He also implied that individualistic nations have a higher need for achievement compared to the collectivist ones. Arguments of this kind have since been dated and regarded as simplistic. For example, when one looks at many collectivist countries which have achieved phenomenal economic performances in the few decades since McClelland wrote his book, one does not find their achievement motive wanting.

The difference between individualistic and collectivist societies may lie behind the ways in which people view achievement and ambition. In the former, an individual strives for his or her own achievement in life; in the latter, the achievement of the group is what matters. For instance, in collectivist countries like Iran, India or Japan, people spend their life's savings on their children's education so that they get good qualifications, find a good job, and marry a person from a respectable background, and so on. In some countries with large extended families, all the family members from grandparents to uncles and cousins and second cousins may collectively support the education of the younger generation. The children's achievement is the achievement of the family as a whole, and their failure brings shame to the whole family. Children in turn try to do well not only for themselves but also for the sake of their family, who will thereby be elevated to a higher status (Tayeb, 1988; Tayeb, 1996a).

Individualism and collectivism have further implications for HRM within the context of employee–employer relationships. According to Hofstede (1980), in collectivist nations employees primarily have a dependent, emotional relationship with their workplace, which looks after their well-being and in return expects loyalty and commitment, this in addition to the labour in exchange for pay contract. In individualistic countries, the employee–employer relationship is primarily contractual, labour is exchanged for pay and that is that. In this connection Segalla (1998), in reporting the findings of a research project that he and his colleagues conducted among a sample of European managers, argues that an intimate relationship exists between a person's sense of well-being and his or her career (that is, his or her relationship with a work group or employer). This relationship is enshrined in a common set of expectations that is known and observed (even if only implicitly) by other employees and, by extension, firms. This expectation set arises from the national culture and not from organisational cultures, defined as a combination of managerial leadership, market needs and recruitment of like-minded employees. To the extent that national cultures are different, the resulting expectation sets must also vary.

However, the implications of national culture in general, and collectivism/individualism in particular, for employee–employer relationships is not simple and straightforward. Because, in part, there are different shades of individualism and collectivism which differentiate between fellow collectivist or fellow individualist nations. Take, for example, three collectivist nations, Japan, India and Iran, societies characterised by, among others, a strong sense of group and community. A typical Japanese, Indian or Iranian person is very loyal to his or her own group or team, and places the interest of the group before his or her own interests. However the size of their in-group distinguishes each of these societies from one another. In Iran the in-group includes not only the nuclear family (parents plus children), but also brothers and sisters and their families, and maybe grandparents as well. In India, in addition to this extended family, close relatives, friends and even clan members are a part of the in-group. In Japan, the company for which the individual works also appears to be included in the in-group.

In addition, there seems to exist in each of us a little bit of both individualism and collectivism, which might surface from time to time and in different circumstances. The French are an individualistic nation but their emphasis on social policies, be it public transport or radio and television services, or shelter for the homeless, shows their collectivism and respect for the common good. In the individualist United Kingdom, a tragedy befalling, for example, a school in a small town brings out the best of community spirit in all the citizens up and down the country. In collectivist India, people can behave in a most individualistic, even cruel, manner towards their fellow citizens, sometimes just on the grounds of caste membership or the degree of poverty and wealth. One needs only to take ride on a crowded train or to walk in the streets to see how harshly some of the poor and low-caste members of society are treated by others.

Japanese culture is perceived both in Japan and in the rest of the world to be characterised by, among other factors, a high degree of collectivism. However, Masakazu, a Japanese sociologist and an expert in aesthetics and drama, challenges this perception. Focusing on the question of individualism in Japanese culture, as opposed to the groupism that is commonly assumed to define it, Masakazu (1994) highlights the prominent role individualistic attitudes and strong personalities have played in the formation of Japan's cultural traditions.

Moreover, there are regional and individual variations within nations regarding their cultural values and attitudes. National boundaries do not always coincide with cultural ones, and even small nations such as Belgium and Switzerland consist of different cultural groupings. And some cultures such as Chinese, Arabic and Kurdish span several national boundaries.

The above discussion serves to remind us that national cultures and their subtle shades make the setting-up and implementation of motivation policies across national boundaries a very complex affair. Generalisations about employees' values, needs and behaviours on the grounds of their culture or level of economic advancement, or any one feature of their society, are at best tentative and shaky.

Performance appraisal, reward and promotion policies

Different nations have evolved different views on these aspects of HRM. In many traditional societies such as some of those in the Middle East, loyalty to superiors takes preference over effective performance of subordinates as measured by the western notion of quality and quantity of output. Moreover, sometimes coherence and harmony in a company are more vital to its smooth running and survival in uncertain economic and political circumstances than setting up performance measures which would encourage competition among employees and departments.

In addition, performance appraisal might have also a foot in other cultural traits of a nation. For example, in Japan performance appraisal is team-based, and it is teams and not individuals which are subsequently rewarded for higher productivity. This arrangement sits well with the predominantly collectivist culture of the country. In the USA and the UK and many other western nations, by contrast, the individual-based performance and reward systems are congruent with their predominantly individualistic cultures.

The assessment of employees' performance and the kind of rewards that they might be given are further influenced by the implicit or explicit social structures, and the consequent distinction made between, for instance, middle-class and working-class people. Tayeb's (1988) study, for example, found that in both English and Indian companies which participated in the research, the performance of managers and other higher-level white-collar employees was assessed by setting targets and objectives to be met within a certain time, and through employee-generated periodical reports. But for blue-collar workers performance was measured by setting daily targets, such as the number of units produced, and inspectors rather than the employees made the assessment as to whether the job was well done.

The rewards for higher performance and punishment for poor quality work were also different for each group of employees. In all the English organisations rewards and punishment for both white-and blue-collar employees took financial forms and were linked to performance. In the Indian organisations the punishment strategies adopted for low-paid manual workers were only non-financial and generally mild, such as shortening annual holidays and failure to promote. Because the government's regulations aimed at maintaining employment and minimum living standards for this group of employees, the managers would not be allowed, for instance, to fire manual workers or reduce their wages under any circumstances, even if they committed gross misconduct and breach of contract. Rewards for managers and other white-collar staff usually took, for tax purposes, non-monetary forms, such as a company house and car, but for manual workers they were financial (their low level of pay would not bring them into taxable bands).

Segalla's (1998) study involving 100 European managers, referred to earlier, showed interesting differences in Europe regarding promotion, remuneration and redundancy decisions. The German sample stood nearly alone in its concern for promoting managers on the basis of objective performance criteria. French managers were at the other extreme in basing promotion on seniority or group loyalty criteria. The German sample again stood alone with its concern that remuneration should be based on measurable individual performance factors. Again the French sample held the extreme opposite belief that remuneration should be based on group, not individual, performance.

English managers most often based staff-reduction decisions on the performance-to-salary ratio. More than 70 per cent of the English respondents would have made redundant a middle-aged, high-salary manager with average performance. In contrast, less than 10 per cent of the German respondents would have discharged the same manager. They favoured discharging young managers who could find jobs more easily, thereby preserving social stability. French respondents were not as concerned with the ratio of performance to salary as the Italians or Spanish. They usually made average-quality employees redundant but were more likely to choose a younger average-quality manager than an older one.

Industrial relations

The multinational company's world is a truly fluid patchwork place with regard to this issue. There are nations in which trade unions do not exist in any form, or if they do it will be on paper only. In practice, employees do not have any protection against potential or actual exploitation or abuse by their employers. In some countries, usually where the right of citizens to be heard and consulted with is recognised, trade unions can flourish. Here, however, the power and influence of trade unions is uneven across the borders. Governments and their industrial relations policies and regulations come and go, at the behest of the electorate, and companies, foreign and domestic alike, have to adapt to these.

In many developing countries, especially those with left-wing tendencies in political and social spheres, such as India, labour laws generally side specifically with employees in an attempt to ensure a minimum standard of living for all the citizens, or even more cynically, in the case of pre-revolutionary Iran, to buy the lower-class people's loyalty to the regime. Moreover, in certain parts of the world, notably the European Union, but also those nations which are signatory to the International Labour Organisation and similar bodies, a supranational layer of labour laws and regulations, notably the Social Chapter, are also in operation.

The extent to which industrial-relations legislation may intrude into the internal affairs of a company also varies from nation to nation, adding yet another layer of complexity to the picture. In some countries like Germany, certain employee rights such as union membership and representation at various levels of decision-making and codetermination are enshrined in the law. In the UK, by contrast, the unions' right to be recognised was until the late 1990s left to the management's good will, and a new law which came into effect in 1998 requires the vote of a majority of employees before the management consents to recognise trade unions in the company. Similarly, minimum wage legislation, which is a part and parcel of industrial relations in the US, was also introduced into the UK labour laws in 1999.

Management of expatriates

Two issues are of relevance to the present chapter with regard to expatriates: why they are sent to subsidiaries, and how well they are prepared for their assignments.

Many multiantional firms, notwithstanding the increasing use of internal networking, still dispatch expatriate managers and other senior staff to their subsidiaries in order to maintain their integration into a coherent whole (see also Chapter 9). Also, as Pucik (1998) points out, most international assignments are still 'demand-driven', filling positions where local know-how is insufficient or where the authority of the centre needs to be upheld in a more direct fashion. In other words, international managers are teachers, transferring new capabilities and maintaining order.

Wyman–Gordon (W–G) is one of four American multinational firms' Scottish subsidiaries in which the present author has recently carried out two separate case studies (Tayeb, 1998; Tayeb and Dott, 2000). The cases demonstrate that even in countries as close as the USA and the UK in terms of national culture and political economic ideology, expatriates in their traditional role as teachers could be a cause of tension and misunderstanding. When W–G was first set up, most senior managers were Americans who had initially been sent with the objective of supervising and directly controlling the subsidiary. As the company grew with increasing profit levels, the Americans were sent more for training purposes. Whatever the purpose, mutual interaction was required between the US managers and the Scottish workforce. As the production manager recalls, the general behaviour and attitudes of the Americans were very different from what they were used to. The following examples were given to illustrate this observation:

> One American manager was sitting in his office; the then Production Control manager approached him with his proposed forge plan on a sheet of paper. The American read it, carefully folded the piece of paper into a paper aeroplane, threw it out the door-way, and said 'follow it'.

> Another American was sitting working at his desk. There was a wall-mounted telephone next to him which kept ringing continuously. This annoyed the American terribly as it was distracting him from his work, and so he wrenched the telephone off the wall and shoved it in his desk drawer.

In another American firm based in Scotland (Tayeb, 1998), the clash of cultures of local employees and expatriates caused a different sort of tension. The first group of a significant number of expatriates were posted to Scotland a few years ago to create a marketing function. These expatriates, about 35 of them, came from the US and some other subsidiaries of the parent company. The Scottish company had reached a stage where they had decided to have a marketing function side by side with their manufacturing base. They needed the marketing expertise, which up until that time was not available in the plant, and they had to get it from other parts of the company that had that expertise.

Although the atmosphere is calm now, when the marketing expatriates arrived there was a great deal of tension, mainly for cultural reasons. The local subsidiary had a long history, and being far enough from the USA it has been left alone, so to speak, to get on with the business. It had been a very successful company, probably the most successful part of the holding group, and the managers strongly believed that it was because they had the freedom to do their own thing, their own way. As a result there was a real resistance, not to mention resentment, at having a large number of expatriates in their midst who came to the company almost overnight. In addition, some of the expatriates were not culturally sensitive, and brought with them their own ways of doing things which were different from the culture of the Scottish plant. For instance, certain people in higher positions liked to be deferred to, whereas American expatriates treated everybody the same. Also, after the establishment of the marketing function by the expatriates, some rules and responsibilities changed. Now marketing was actually dictating things to manufacturing and R&D and so forth. There was a real feeling that these 'outsiders, these upstarts', were telling the local employees what to do. This was not liked at all and created a great deal of resentment among the workforce.

Another cause of tension was the pay and benefit differentiation between home employees and expatriates. The latter, for various reasons to do with various deductions, the maintenance of expatriates' US lifestyle in Scotland, and other contractual obligations, would receive a relatively generous salary and housing benefits and were provided with company cars. Most local managers did not have company cars, only directors did. Local managers were therefore resentful because they were working side by side with the expatriates at the same level, but they did not have any of these extra benefits. So there was a great deal of tension. This disappeared largely because many of the expatriates went back home and were not as visible anymore. Also, the expatriates started communicating better with the workforce and informing them of the reasons they were there and their plans for the future.

The teaching role of expatriates might change, however, in the future and these sorts of tensions might also disappear. As Pucik (1998) argues, with less need for knowledge transfer from the centre, many expatriates will be students, not teachers. Coming from all over the organisation they will learn through experience about market and cultural differences while developing long-lasting networks of relationships. The HR support system will have to adjust to this by linking policies and practices more tightly to the purpose of cross-border assignments.

The ways in which multinational firms manage their expatriates, in terms of, for instance, pre-assignment preparation, and post-assignment support, are different from one another. And there appears to be a home-country imprint on differences between companies in this regard, which may also have implications for their performance. Tung's (1984) survey of a sample of American and Japanese multinationals and their human resource management practices regarding their employees abroad found that, on the whole, Japanese companies had a better record compared to their American counterparts in terms of their employees' performance, among other things. She found that such characteristics as employees' high level of commitment, managers' familiarity with and understanding of their subordinates' personal and family circumstances, extensive training programmes, including a spell of time spent abroad, a long-term perspective regarding employee performance and attitudes, all helped to create a better record of employee performance abroad compared to the American firms studied, which displayed almost the opposite of their Japanese counterparts on the above issues.

The present author would like to argue that, compared to the Americans, the Japanese employees' sociocultural setting back home has provided them with a higher repertoire of modes of behaviour, and hence greater flexibility, which stands them in good stead when abroad. Their managers both back home and in the foreign subsidiaries also display a greater repertoire of human resource management strategies and practices. The overall results put Japanese multinational companies in a better position compared to their American competitors.

This point is further supported by the findings of Tung's (1988) subsequent surveys, where she compared Japanese and American multinationals' expatriate management strategies and practices with those of a sample of European ones. Here she found that American multinationals fared worse compared to both their Japanese and European counterparts. The Americans had a much higher failure rate, which was found to have roots in their shorter time-perspective and less positive attitudes to and understanding of foreign cultures. In other words, sociocultural characteristics of the home base of American multinationals had constrained their performance as far as expatriate HRM practices were concerned; whereas the societal traits of their European and Japanese competitors had enhanced their performance abroad.

SUMMARY

This chapter has presented widely-used definitions of HRM and its hard and soft models, and discussed the culture-bound nature of the concept of HRM itself. The implications of national culture for HRM policies has been explored, including practices such as recruitment, training, job expectations and motivation, performance appraisal and promotion criteria. Issues such as industrial relations and management of expatriates have also been examined with regard to the effects of national culture. Variations on all these practices in certain countries were cited to illustrate the impact of culture on them, and, by implication the challenges that they pose to firms with operations in different parts of the world.

A distinction is made between HRM *policies* and HRM *practices*, and it is argued that whereas international firms tend to achieve HRM integration with regard to HRM policies, they are inclined to differentiate their HRM practices to suit local circumstances.

9 Organisational Culture

INTRODUCTION

Organisational culture is a concept which, like its two constituent parts, is difficult to define. Schein (1985), a writer who has contributed most significantly to the study of organisational culture, proposed his own definition after a brief critical assessment of other writers. He argued that organisational culture should be viewed as a property of an independently defined stable social unit. Organisational culture refers to basic assumptions and beliefs that are shared by members of an organisation. These operate unconsciously, and define in a basic 'taken-for-granted' fashion an organisation's view of itself and its environment. These assumptions and views are based on shared experiences and have worked for a sufficiently long time to be taken for granted and be dropped out of awareness. Organisational culture, in this sense, is a learned product of group experience and is therefore to be found only where there is a definable group with a significant history.

In the same vein, Denison (1990) sees organisational culture as a code, a logic, and a system of structured behaviours and meanings that have stood the test of time and serve as a collective guide to future adaptation and survival.

Similarly, Tunstall (1983) describes corporate culture as a general constellation of beliefs, mores, customs, value systems, behavioural norms and ways of doing business that are unique to each corporation, that set a pattern for corporate activities and actions, and that describe the implicit emergent patterns of behaviour and emotions characterising life in the organisation. There have also been studies which have explored and discussed the surface levels of culture (for example rites, stories, legends and so forth) and examined their relationship to deeper levels of values and beliefs (see for instance Martin *et al.*, 1983; Sathe, 1983; Trice and Beyer, 1984).

The origins of corporate culture could be traced, among other things, to the founder or founders of the organisation – their value systems, attitudes, beliefs, philosophy, and likes and dislikes. For instance, the founders might value hard work, honesty and punctuality, and believe in caring for employees and being responsive to their customers' needs. They bring these values and beliefs with them to the organisations they set up. Many internationally known multinationals such as Toyota and

Hewlett-Packard owe much of their current culture and philosophy to their original owners. Also, in addition to the founders' values and beliefs, organisational culture as a living entity reflects the learning and retention that have occurred over time, solutions to problems which have worked well enough to be considered valid and therefore to be taught to new members as the correct way to perceive, think and feel in relation to those problems (Schein, 1985; Denison, 1990).

However, following Hofstede (1994), and paraphrasing his argument, it is important to note that there is a distinction between the values of founders and leaders, and the corporation in general, and those of ordinary employees. Organisational culture creates the values, the symbols, the heroes and the rituals that constitute the daily practices of the organisation's members. Members adapt their personal values to the organisation's needs to a limited extent only; a workplace, as a rule, is not a 'total institution' like a prison or a mental hospital. The values of employees cannot be changed by an employer, because they were acquired when the employees were children.

To employ a metaphor one can visualise, the employees would leave their life-long value systems at the door when they enter the premises of their workplace in the morning, and pick them up again when they leave in the afternoon. While at work, they may follow the *practices* advocated by their employers, but they cannot be coerced to believe deep down in the same *values* as theirs. However, as Hofstede (1994) points out, sometimes an employer can activate latent values of employees, like a desire for initiative and creativity, by allowing practices which provide the employees with appropriate opportunities.

NATIONAL CULTURE AND ORGANISATIONAL CULTURE

To what extent are the values, attitudes and patterns of behaviour that managers and other employees display in an organisation rooted in their national cultural background? And to what extent in their organisation's culture? This is a very difficult question to answer.

On a general level, it is possible to discern differences between organisations around the world which are compatible with their home-country characteristics. Japan's Toyota and Nissan companies are in many ways different from Germany's Volkswagen and France's Renault manufacturers. There are some characteristics that Toyota and Nissan have which betray their 'Japaneseness': harmonious industrial relations, company-based trades unions, quality circles, just-in-time and so forth. We see the first of these management practices in the German company as well, but not the others, certainly not to the same extent. Moreover, the fact that not all companies in the same country look alike or behave alike says something about their uniqueness, about their own specific organisational culture.

Just as each individual member of a society shares some characteristics in common with others in the society, and yet retains unique personal traits, each individual organisation has its own unique culture and 'personality', while at the same time it shares many characteristics in common with all other organisations in the country as a whole. The differing corporate cultures of Hewlett-Packard, AT&T and other major American firms, described by Morgan (1986), are good examples here. Disentanglement of national culture from organisational culture is a topic which has posed a formidable challenge to the researchers of comparative organisations, a challenge which has not yet been fully met.

In a study conducted in Holland and Denmark (Hofstede *et al.*, 1990), Hofstede and his colleagues attempted to address the issue of organisational vs national culture. They found considerable *differences in values*, in the sense of broad, non-specific feelings, such as good and evil, between the two national cultures (comparing otherwise similar people). Among organisational cultures, the opposite was the case: they found considerable *differences in practices* for people who held about the *same values*.

However, their study did not quite succeed in separating the influences of organisational culture from that of national culture on employees' work-related values and attitudes. As the authors themselves point out:

> All in all, having gone out to study organizational value differences and having done this in two countries for reasons of convenience, we seem to have mainly caught national value differences. (Hofstede *et al.*, 1990, p. 300)

There are, of course, sub-cultures within an organisation, as is indeed the case with national cultures. Organisational sub-cultures could for instance be based on functions, such as the marketing department, or on members' occupations, such as a managerial culture. In multinational firms an added layer superimposes itself on corporate and functional and professional cultures in the form of a subsidiary's own culture. In addition, both functional and professional cultures vary from one country to another, reflecting each country's general patterns of doing things, including business activities. This makes the disentanglement of the corporate culture and national cultures of both the parent company and its subsidiaries a very complicated process indeed. In fact, it is very difficult, if not impossible, to speak of one organisational culture for a large multinational firm with multiple outfits sprinkled around the world.

What founding fathers of a multinational company did and advocated loses a great deal of its potency and character by the time it percolates down and is spread across the globe. Moreover, the learning and retention process, as one of the pillars of culture-building in an organisation, is not of course identical across subsidiaries, far from it. In addition, some societal institutions and characteristics, such as for instance the industrial relations culture, have a strong influence on the ways in which certain things are done within an organisation. The 'them and us' attitude which still bedevils industrial relations in the United Kingdom, and which is a reflection of the class-based and class-conscious culture of the country as a whole, has for a long time been a constant feature of organisational culture in many British companies.

Most Britons are conscious of class differentiation, and almost everybody one speaks with can place themselves in one class or another. Family background, education, and even accent, betray people's social class. The class hierarchy consists broadly of an upper class (a very small proportion of the total population), middle class and working class, but there are subtle gradations within classes; even though there is no sharp and rigid division between these strata and there is movement between classes. Tayeb (1988), in a comparative study of organisations which included a sample of English manufacturing companies, found that the differences between shopfloor workers and white-collar employees, especially managers, inside the participating organisations appeared to be a reflection of the social structures and systems of the society as a whole. The managers considered themselves to be members of the middle class, which shares in the ownership and participates in the control of the means of production, and the manual workers saw themselves as members of the working class exploited by the former. In most cases, the relationship between management and workers was characterised by mistrust and misunderstanding, emanating from a conflict of interests between the two classes.

There were also other more tangible manifestations of the class-based differentiation of the workforce present in the companies. The managers and other white-collar employees had greater advantages over the manual workers in many respects, such as power, status, pay, physical working conditions, eating places, rules for lunch and tea breaks, and holidays. Shopfloor workers, on the other hand, were subject to a tighter control at work. They had to clock in and out at specific times, and in some of the companies which produced chemicals and drugs they were subject to physical search every time they left the company premises.

Ten years later, in another study involving the Scottish subsidiaries of three American firms, Tayeb found the British 'them and us' attitude was still very much alive (Tayeb and Dott, 2000). The managing director of one of the companies admitted that a 'them and us' attitude existed between management and workers: 'This is an ingrained conception that the local people have – always having seen management as a body of people with no name to it'. Although the company has always had a single canteen for all employees, there are other visible signs which support the distinction between management and the workforce, especially manual workers. For example, they have distinctly designated car parks, with senior management car spaces placed in ascending order at the front entrance to the building; each with his/her own space based on an implicit understanding by all employees that the space goes with the position they hold in the company. Thus, as employees get promoted up through the organisation, they respectively move up in their car park spaces. The car parks, as the production manager recalled, have always been organised in this way since the beginning and were even reorganised to accommodate the new arrangements when the main reception was relocated a few years ago.

This situation contrasts sharply with the industrial relations culture, and its implications for organisational culture, in Japan. Japanese society, unlike in many other modern countries, is not stratified horizontally by class or caste. The overall picture of the society is that of vertical stratification by institution or group of institutions. For example, a shopfloor technician does not identify himself or herself with all the technicians in the country or with the working class in general. He or she identifies himself or herself with his or her work organisation and all those people who work below and above him or her within it. As Nakane (1973) puts it:

> ... even if social classes like those in Europe can be detected in Japan, and even if something vaguely resembling those classes that are illustrated in the textbooks of Western sociology can also be found in Japan, the point is that it does not really reflect the social structure. In Japanese society it is really not a matter of workers' struggles against capitalist or managers but of Company A ranged against Company B. (p. 90)

This vertical class structure appears to have been reflected at the national level in Japanese industrial relations and trade unionism, and at the organisational level in employee–management relationships.

Trade unions in Japan are company-based and one of their principal characteristics is that both white and blue-collar workers are organised into the same union. Another contributory factor to this 'side-by-side', rather than 'them and us' feature of trade unionism and employee–management relationships, can be found in a relatively recent history of the country. Shirai (1983) reckons that the origins of enterprise unionism go back to the 1920s, and they are sustained to date because workers prefer this form of representation to any other on offer. This is principally due to their enterprise consciousness, itself brought about because of Japan's heavy dependence on imports of energy, raw materials and food. This has made, he argues, most union leaders acutely conscious of the competitiveness and productivity of their industries. Most of them believe that in the long run the employment security and improvement of working and living conditions of their members crucially depends upon how their industry improves its position in changing world markets. As a result, the enterprise unions generally have a cooperative attitude toward management, although in substantive terms they appear to serve their members well.

The character of unions and management is thus moulded into the company culture, and the relationship between the two sides, if they can be separated as two sides, are based on cooperation and harmony.

Because of the societal differences of the kind discussed above, the character of organisational culture in each subsidiary of a multinational firm is substantially different from the others. NCR's plant in Scotland (Tayeb, 1998) illustrates this point further. A few years ago, when NCR's holding company was taken over by AT&T, the new parent-company management introduced a programme of common bond. The idea was to create a common identity within each subsidiary and throughout the company worldwide, and to remove or at least reduce status differentiation among the workforce. But some of the means and the language used to convey such an idea met with resistance and challenge in Scotland.

For instance, according to the new management style, managers and employees were now to be 'coaches' and 'associates'. At a conference in New York where the programme was launched, the objection to such terms by a representative from Scotland reflects the cultural problems inherent in the use of such a language. He said: 'Excuse me, this may seem strange to you but if you say coach to somebody in Scotland, they don't think about the team coach or the football, they think of the bus that brings them to work.'

On a more serious level, the common bond programme also caused serious offence to the workforce. As part of the programme there was to be explicit emphasis on such concepts as respect for individuals, dedication to helping customers, highest standards of integrity, innovation and teamwork. To bring the message home, a one-day mass meeting was organised in a special venue and the programme was introduced to the workforce. Posters were put up everywhere in the company premises to remind people of this new creed. The effect on the workforce, however, was negative. This was not because people did not agree with what such concepts signified. But they had been offended that the new parent company had felt it necessary to tell them such ideals should be aimed and pursued in the company. As one of those who was present at the meeting put it:

A lot of people, and I include myself, said 'I really am offended, in fact almost insulted, that they feel they've got to do this with us'. Because my firm belief, being in this job and having been in it all the years I've been here, that unless we operated for example, with integrity, we wouldn't have lasted. The company wouldn't have lasted the 50 years that it's been in Dundee. If we had not applied the principles of the common bond across the board during those 50 years, then we wouldn't be celebrating the 50th anniversary this year. So that came over from the US and I don't think it was well received. I think a lot of people said this is an absolute nonsense, I mean coming to teach us at this stage in the game is just crazy stuff, it's quite offensive. I think they consider it in the US to be still alive and kicking, but as far as I'm concerned, we operate the way that we've always operated, and that probably incorporates what they call the common bond.

Most people did not call each other coaches and associates in the subsidiary, and the posters on the walls were for all intents and purposes ignored. AT&T and NCR parted ways two years later.

ORGANISATIONAL CULTURE AND PERFORMANCE

Many researchers and writers have argued that an organisation's culture has an important impact on its performance, quite apart from its objectives, or material or structural characteristics. Denison (1990), for example, shows in his extensive case study project that structures, strategies and their implementations are rooted in the basic beliefs and values of an organisation and present both limits and opportunities for what may be accomplished. He goes on to say that the effectiveness of an organisation must be studied as a cultural phenomenon linking assumptions and shared values with management practices and strategies in order to understand a firm's adaptation over time. However, he continues, rather than simply argue that culture causes effectiveness, one must consider the ways in which an organisation's culture is shaped through past successes and failures. The nature of a particular culture is, therefore, a reflection of the original strategies of the founders of the firm, as well as the learning and retention that have occurred over time.

Nicholaidis (1992) in a study of organisational culture and performance of 105 British companies, 99 Greek companies and 41 Greek firms based in London, found that harmonising corporate culture with both nation- and industry-specific environmental factors motivates excellence in corporate performance. In a far less academically vigorous work, Peters and Waterman (1982) also attributed the high performance of certain companies to their specific strong organisational culture. However, some of these firms, notwithstanding their 'excellent' organisational culture, were unable to sustain their level of performance a few years after the above book was published.

Nevertheless, organisational culture can be conceived of as a control and integration mechanism in widely differentiated firms, such as multinationals, which can be used to benefit the company as a whole if employed judiciously. As Hofstede (1998) argues:

> Although nobody has found – or is likely to find – a simple one-to-one relationship of any aspect of organizational culture with organizational performance, there is little doubt that organizational culture affects performance; in the long run it may be the one decisive influence for the survival or fall of the organization – although this is difficult to prove, if only because the necessary longitudinal analyses are hardly feasible. (p. 491)

GLOBAL MINDSET AS A CULTURE-BUILDING INTEGRATIVE PROCESS

Creating and incorporating a global mindset, as opposed to an ethnocentric one, in a multinational corporate culture is one way of spreading

certain values and of unifying some aspects of members' thought processes and actions within the confines of the corporation. Govindarajan
and Gupta (1998a), whose paper is drawn on in the next three para-
graphs, define an organisation's mindset, its theory of the world, as the
aggregated mindset of the collective adjusted for the distribution of
power and mutual influence among the people making up this collective.

'Mindset', the authors go on to say, refers to the cognitive filters
through which we, as individuals or organisations, observe and make
sense of the world. None of us is omniscient; we are selective in what we
observe and biased in how we interpret what we observe. We acquire
these cognitive filters through a process of learning from experience.
Thus the greater the diversity in the experiences of two individuals or
organisations, the more likely it is that their mindsets will be different.

A firm's mindset shapes perceptions in virtually every area: what the
nature and size of the opportunity space is; who the customer is; how
customer needs are changing; who the firm really competes with; what
technologies are central to the industry; and so forth. Thus, a firm's
mindset has a direct and determining impact on what strategies it pur-
sues and what investments it makes to implement them. A global mindset rests on a foundation of openness. An organisation with a global
mindset operates on the premise that cultures can be different without
being better or worse than one another. Such an organisation dedicates
itself to becoming well-informed about different value systems, different norms of behaviour and different assumptions regarding reality. It
accepts diversity and heterogeneity as natural and as a source of opportunities and strengths rather than as a necessary evil.

This acceptance of diversity does not imply that the organisation with
a global mindset becomes a prisoner of diversity and closes itself to the
possibility of working across cultures or transferring innovations and
superior practices from one culture to another. On the contrary, the
openness inherent in a global mindset implies an openness to change
over time – in one's own culture as well as in that of others. As Percy
Barnevik, ABB's architect and first chief executive, observed astutely:
'Global managers have exceptionally open minds. They respect how
different countries do things and they have the imagination to appreci-
ate why they do them that way. But they are also incisive; they push the
limits of the culture' (quoted in Govindarajan and Gupta, 1998a, p. 2).

One of the ways in which multinationals could create and strengthen
their global mindset and perspective is by appointing multicultural
senior executive boards. Harvey and Buckley (1997) point to a growing
trend among multinational firms in this respect. Asea Brown Boveri

(ABB), a Swedish–Swiss electrical engineering firm, has a board of directors consisting of eight individuals from four different nationalities; an executive committee of eight with five managers from countries other than Sweden or Switzerland. Royal Dutch/Shell has over 38 nationalities represented in its London headquarters and nearly as diverse a work-force in its operating units throughout the world (Copeland, 1995; Pechter, 1993; Thornhill, 1993). Japanese multinationals such as Mat-sushita and Sony have taken similar steps to increase the cultural diversity of their senior managers (Harvey and Buckley, 1997).

At the other end of the executive spectrum, Unilever is a good exam-ple of a company that commences the globalisation process fairly early in a manager's career through mechanisms such as international place-ments and a management training centre that brings together 300 to 400 managers from all over the world each year. Moreover, for many years Unilever has followed a policy whereby most people who rise to the top of any business unit should have worked in at least two coun-tries and should speak at least one language besides their native tongue (Govindarajan and Gupta, 1998a).

Although global mobility is an important way in which the oppor-tunities to develop a global mindset might be enhanced, such a mobil-ity is not always possible or desirable (Pucik, 1998). Socioeconomic and cultural trends around the world are increasing barriers to mobil-ity. Dual-career families, parental care needs, children's educational needs and reduced incentives for moving because of the equalisation of economic opportunities are all factors that may diminish employees' desire to seek out international assignments. In response, global organisations will have to become more creative in finding alternatives to mobility, especially for senior managers, eliminating traditional country-based job boundaries and taking advantage of state-of-the-art communications.

Training can also make a significant contribution to the creation and retention of a global mindset. The formation of the peer group on courses which bring together representatives from all parts of the com-pany; choice of the right content and case material, the style of the courses and the messages they convey about the international orienta-tion of the business – all are important and productive. However, as Vineall (1988) argues, training courses can do little on their own. If the messages are inconsistent with the way the corporation operates, they can do harm. But as a complement to an organisation with a clear sense of direction and commitment to an international style of operation, their contribution is enormous.

Organisational culture can sometimes be used as a substitute for the local culture in an attempt to overcome some of its dysfunctions, for example, a weak work ethic, corruption or dishonesty. Conversely, creation of a cultural synergy (Adler, 1990) enables senior managers to incorporate in the company's own culture the desirable aspects of the local national culture, such as group-orientation, commitment, honesty and hard work, where appropriate and possible. Particularly important, and not quickly achieved, as Vineall (1988) points out, is the right relationship between corporate culture and the national cultures in which individuals live. A wise company will not see its corporate culture as something which challenges or replaces, or even transcends, the local manager's identity as a German or Canadian or Nigerian. Ideally, managers should feel fully nationals of their own country, yet equally fully members of the corporate club.

But, can one change employees' cultural attitudes and values? Is culture malleable? Attitude theories suggest that people's attitudes and behaviours can be changed through communication and persuasion (Petty, 1981; Kleinke, 1984), cultural shock (Hofstede, 1978) and sustained discontinuity (Mangham, 1978). As Silverman (1970, p. 135) puts it, 'If the reality of the social world is socially sustained, then it follows that reality is socially changed – by action of [humans]'. Cultural change and cultural synergy in an organisation can therefore be initiated, developed and maintained largely by the daily actions of those who run the business – by what they say, by what they do. Bate (1982) also argues in the same vein and offers a possible way to introduce the change:

> Perhaps the initial step would be for the change agent to attempt to raise the parties' awareness of their culture – the taken-for-granted meanings that they share and collectively maintain, and which inhibit the development of effective problem solving activities. (p. 27)

This is a pertinent point. One can understand other people's points of view and expectations within an organisational setting, as indeed in other situations, only when one knows where one's own ideas and deeply-held views come from. However, such points do not appear to have been taken on board by many international integration programmes. According to many researchers, few people really know their own cultural values until those values are threatened by an outside culture, and, as Segalla (1998) points out, this may be one reason why so many cultural integration programmes start with grand expectations and goodwill but end in indifference or resentment.

The basic requirement of any international human resources integration programme is a very deep examination of the local cultural values relating to human resources policy. This is important because all cultures accumulate basic expectations about what employers and employees can or cannot demand from each other. Most international managers will have experienced these expectation differences at first hand. Unfortunately, while large sums are often spent on training and 'cultural change' programmes, few managers are willing to commit much time, effort or money to understanding their own expectation sets.

Segalla (1998) then cites an example of one large French multinational which created an international management programme for young 'high-potential' managers in its European network. An important goal was to create an international cadre of young managers who would help integrate the company's many recent acquisitions into a tightly organised pan-European organisation. Not only was the definition of 'high potential' different from country to country, but despite detailed written guidelines those chosen were disappointing to the headquarters staff. During an eight-day training seminar in France many failed to understand what the programme was really all about. They maintained their normal expectation sets. Some felt that they were simply starting an expatriate assignment without all the perks. (There were no supplemental salary benefits during the two-year foreign assignment that was part of the programme.) Others saw themselves as 'high potentials' being groomed for higher posts in their home countries. They did not seem to grasp the idea that they were to be the backbone of a network of managers who could connect the various parts of the company. Eight days was too short a time for the trainees to reconsider their expectation sets in light of the company's attempt to create an integrated organisation.

Finally, expatriate managers, although they are assumed by many to be on their way out, being gradually replaced by networking, are still major players in the international scene. They fulfil a significant role in spreading around the parent company's values and preferences, both directly as 'teachers' and trainers, and indirectly as role models.

SUMMARY

Organisational culture is another aspect of an international firm which is likely to be affected by the national cultures of the firm's sub-units and subsidiaries located in different countries. The combined contribution of the two constructs to the final make up of the firm, although difficult to disentangle and study individually and even more so to measure, is argued to be nonetheless real.

In this chapter we have presented major definitions of organisational culture and explored its effects on a company's performance. It has also been argued that international firms tend to use organisational culture as an integrative mechanism and to reinforce its effectiveness by fostering a global mindset in its workforce, especially among those in positions of power and influence.

Expatriates are also deployed as culture-builders who move among and between 'outposts' to foster common companywide values and beliefs, in addition to their normal roles as trainers and overseers of the proper conduct of business.

10 Summary and Conclusions

This book has attempted to put together in one volume major issues and arguments, supported by available empirical evidence and theoretical models, which concern the birth and growth of international firms and the challenges that they face in their sometimes worldwide environment.

Chapter 1 focused on the discussion of competitiveness of nations and the socio-political factors which might enhance or hinder it. It was argued that, notwithstanding some instances of decoupling of nations and companies, the fates of the two are intertwined. Nations provide launching pads for their home-grown companies through various political, economic and educational policies and practices, as well as their centuries-old cultural values, traditions and customs. Companies cannot normally launch themselves into the international arena without a platform from which they can be powerfully propelled. Some of these 'platforms', in comparison with the rest of the world, have done a better job of preparing and launching their home-grown firms into the international marketplace where they compete successfully with other firms.

The first chapter built on Porter's (1990) model by focusing on and exploring major socio-political roots of the inequalities between nations. Examples of unsuccessful as well as successful nations were cited to illustrate why some countries do not have any significant presence through their business firms in the competitive markets of today.

Both on economic measures such as the size of an economy, its growth rate and per capita income, and non-economic indicators such as health, life-expectancy and literacy rate, Germany, France, the United States, Japan, Canada, the United Kingdom, Hong Kong, Singapore, South Korea, Taiwan and many other OECD countries have left other nations far behind. Many countries located in central and western Asia, Africa and some parts of Latin America still have a long way to go. There are also some very hopeful and promising nations such as Hungary, the Czech Republic, Poland, China and Brazil in between these two groups which are set to join the frontrunners in the near future.

In terms of competitiveness, according to an annual survey by the International Institute for Management Development (IMD), the United States continues to be the most competitive nation in the world, followed

Table 10.1   Top-ten competitive nations (rank order)

Country	1998	1999
United States	1	1
Singapore	2	2
Finland	5	3
Luxembourg	9	4
Netherlands	4	5
Switzerland	7	6
Hong Kong	3	7
Denmark	8	8
Germany	14	9
Canada	10	10

Source: IMD, cited in *The Economist*, 24 April 1999, p. 7.

by a few others, all predictably from the so-called Triad regions. Table 10.1 shows how these nations stood in 1998 and 1999 in this respect. One of the major factors contributing to the success of these nations has been their liberal economic and trade policies. As Govindarajan and Gupta (1998b), along with many other like-minded scholars, point out, economic liberalisation promotes competition, efficiency, innovation, new capital investment and faster economic growth. Not surprisingly, the embrace of market mechanisms has allowed the developing economies of the world to start catching up with the advanced economies. Taiwan, Hong Kong and Singapore, some of the world's poorest countries in the 1950s, already count among the advanced economies. Despite the short-term disruptions caused by the recent Asian financial crisis, the projections of long-term growth for the region are still valid.

Other, even larger, economies are advancing, notably China. Having sustained a better than 10 per cent annual growth rate since 1980, China has already transformed itself into the third largest economy in the world, at least on a purchasing power parity basis, and seems poised to overtake Japan in the not-too-distant future.

As was discussed in Chapter 2, the opening of borders to trade, investment and technology transfers not only creates new market opportunities for companies but also enables competitors from abroad to enter their home markets. As competition intensifies, it fuels the race among competitors to serve customers around the world, to capture economies of scale, to exploit the cost-reducing or quality-enhancing potentials of optimal locations, and to tap technological advancements wherever they may occur (Govindarajan and Gupta, 1998b).

However, many economies are still run on closed- or semi-closed-door models, which not only deprive their peoples of quality products at competitive prices, but also in most part unduly shelter their home-grown companies from a healthy competition which could season them for the race in international markets. The *Financial Times*' 1997 list of 'The World's Top 500 Companies', based on market capitalisation, does not include a single entry from India – a protected economy, which in spite of its slow and gradual liberalisation is still far behind many of its fellow Asian neighbours to the north and east, notably China, Japan, and the so-called four Asian tigers.

The protectionist policies of many developing countries are, among other things, rooted in their deep suspicion of foreigners because of colonial and other forms of foreign domination in the past. India, Iran and even China, for example, which had until relatively recently firmly closed their economies to liberally conducted foreign trade and investment, have ample reasons, real and imagined, to be careful.

Chapter 3 discussed internal characteristics and core competencies of international companies as major contributing factors to their competitiveness and success. It was argued that although some nations might provide the potential wherewithal for internationalisation, it is ultimately up to the individual firm's ability to take advantage of and build on it. However, there is still a role for national political and cultural factors here. Companies may, for instance, be quite capable of managing their affairs, given a competent and educated workforce, but if such a resource is not available in sufficient quantity then they may not be able to do much about it. They can of course invest in the training of local people or invite foreign experts and expatriates to come and work for them, but this is not always possible or even permissible for various reasons, usually of a political kind, in certain countries.

Chapter 4 focused on the motives for internationalisation and the forms that it might take. Here again major political and cultural factors which could shape the internationalisation process were discussed. It was also argued that these factors could, in addition, set limits to the extent of internationalisation and globalisation of both producers and consumers. There are many nations which are off-limits as far as globalisation is concerned, they are either shunned by the international community or are in self-imposed 'exile', mainly on political grounds. Also, the control of mass communication media, including those that appear to be borderless and uncontrollable, such as the Internet and satellite-based television and radio, is still in the hands of the state in many countries, again mainly for political reasons. This limits local consumers' awareness of and exposure to the products and services which exist beyond their country's physical borders. It also limits the scope and ability of the providers of goods and services to tap potential markets in many parts of the world.

Chapters 5 to 9 brought the analysis to the company level and discussed major managerial issues such as strategy development, the interface with the external environment, organisational design and culture and human resource management, bearing in mind the broader political and cultural contexts within which international firms operate. At the strategic level, it was argued, some companies, thanks to their home-country's foreign and economic policies and practices, are in a far better position to expand into foreign markets compared to their less 'fortunate' counterparts. The latter's hands are sometimes tied even if their managers are equally competent and technically knowledgeable. Inadequate information and physical infrastructure in their home countries, for instance, can and do hamper their efforts to embark on proper investment planning beyond their immediate future. Such inadequacies not only affect domestic firms, but also the foreign firms located in those countries.

At the interface level, relationships with suppliers, customers and other relevant actors are all affected by the sociocultural and political characteristics of the nations with whom international firms do business. Marketing, advertising, customer relations and negotiations are particularly sensitive to people's cultural values and beliefs and can be sources of embarrassment and even breakdown of business dealings if handled improperly.

At the internal organisational and human resource management level, international firms encounter a variety of challenges, rooted in their multicultural multifaceted nature. There are areas of their management, notably the so-called 'hard' universal aspects, where it is possible to converge policies and practices across national boundaries. But there are also 'soft' culture-specific aspects, notably the management of their workforce, where divergences of styles and methods are more practical and fruitful. The culturally and geographically-induced differentiation of policies and practices and the integration of subsidiaries and affiliates required for the maintenance of a unified overall direction, however, go hand in hand and not in competition with one another. Moreover, this coexistence appears to run alongside the culture-specific/ universal axis – differentiation takes place largely in the culture-specific functions of the company, such as HRM; integration in the universal, culture-free functions, such as strategy development.

The organisational culture, dispatch of expatriates, establishment of intra-unit networks, and development of a global mindset among the workforce are among the major devices that international companies employ to respond adequately to their diverse constituencies and to integrate effectively their diverse constituents into a recognisable whole. Modern technologies, notably electronic telecommunications, greatly help this process along.

Bibliography

Abegglen, J. C. and Stalk, G. (1985) *Kaish: The Japanese Corporation* (New York: Basic Books).

Adler, N. J. (1990) *Dimensions of Organizational Behavior*, 2nd edn (Boston: Kent Publishing).

Ali, A. J. (1995) 'Cultural Discontinuity and Arab Management Thought', *International Studies of Management and Organization*, 25(3), 7–21.

Altany, D. (1989) 'Culture Clash', *Industry Week*, 2 October, 13–20.

Amsden, A. H. (1989) *Asia's Next Giant* (Oxford: Oxford University Press).

Arnold, G. (1989) *The Third World Handbook* (London: Cassell).

Bakhtari, H. (1995) 'Cultural Effects on Management Style', *International Studies of Management and Organization*, 25(3), 97–118.

Bani-Asadi, H. (1984) 'Interactive Planning on the Eve of the Iranian Revolution, PhD dissertation, University of Pennsylvania.

Barnett, C. (1972) *The Collapse of British Power* (London: Eyre Methuen).

Bartholomew, S. (1997) 'The Globalization of Technology: A Socio-cultural Perspective', in J. Howells and J. Michie (eds), *Technology, Innovation and Competitiveness* (Cheltenham: Edward Elgar), 37–64.

Bartlett, C. A. and Ghoshal, S. (1989) *Managing Across Borders: The Transnational Solution* (London: Century Business).

Bate, P. (1982) 'Impact of Organisational Culture on Approaches to Organisational Problem-solving', paper presented to the Conference on Qualitative Approaches to Organisations, University of Bath, 19–21 April.

Beckermann, W. (1956) 'Distance and the Pattern of Intra-European Trade', *Review of Economics and Statistics*, 28, 31–40.

Beechler, S. and Yang, J. Z. (1994) 'The Transfer of Japanese-style Management to American Subsidiaries: Contingencies, Constraints, and Competencies', *Journal of International Business Studies*, 25, 467–91.

Beer, M. and Spector, B. (1985) 'Corporate-wide Transformations in Human Resource Management', in R. E. Walton and P. R. Lawrence (eds), *Human Resource Management: Trends and Challenges* (Boston, Mass.: Harvard Business School Press), 219–53.

Bell, J. and Young, S. (1998) 'Towards an Integrative Framework of the Internationalization of the Firm', in G. Hooley, R. Loveridge and D. Wilson (eds), *Internationalization: Process, Context and Markets* (London: Macmillan), 5–28.

Bilkey, W. J. (1978) 'An Attempted Integration of the Literature on the Export Behavior of Firms', *Journal of International Business Studies*, 9(1), 33–46.

Birkinshaw, J. M. (1995) '*Entrepreneurship in Multinational Corporations: The Initiative Process in Canadian Subsidiaries*', unpublished doctoral dissertation, Western Business School.

Birkinshaw, J. M. and Hood, N. (1998) 'The Determinants of Subsidiary Mandates and Subsidiary Initiative: A Three-country Study', in G. Hooley, R. Loveridge and D. Wilson (eds), *Internationalization: Process, Context and Markets* (London: Macmillan).

Briggs, P. (1988) 'The Japanese at Work: Illusions of the Ideal', *Industrial Relations Journal*, 19, 24–30.

Brooke, M. Z. (1996) *International Management: A Review of Strategies and Operations*, 3rd edn (Cheltenham: Stanley Thornes Publishers).

Buchholz, R. A. (1991) 'Corporate Responsibility and the Good Society: From Economics to Ecology', *Business Horizons*, July–August, 19–31.

Buckley, P. J. (1988) 'The Limits of Explanation: Testing the Internationalization Theory of the Multinational Enterprise', *Journal of International Business Studies*, 19(2), 181–4.

Buckley, P. J. and Casson, M. (1976) *The Future of Multinational Enterprise* (London: Macmillan).

Burns, T. and Stalker, G. M. (1961) *The Management of Innovation*, (London: Tavistock).

Campbell, N. C. G. (1988) 'Competitive Advantage from Rational Marketing: The Japanese Approach', in A. Pettigrew, (ed.), *Competitiveness and the Management Process* (Oxford: Blackwell), 230–44.

Cavausgil, S. T. (1980) 'On the Internationalization Process of the Firm', *European Research*, 8(6), 273–81.

Chassang, G. and Reitter, R. (1998) 'Steering Between Chaos and Tyranny', *Financial Times*, 7 March, survey p. 12.

Chaudhuri, K. N. (1971) *The Economic Development of India under the East India Company 1814–1858* (Cambridge: Cambridge University Press).

Chaudhuri, K. K. (1981) 'Workers' Participation in India: A Review of Studies, 1950–1980', Indian Institute of Management, Calcutta, working paper no. 41.

Child, J. (1972) 'Organizational Structure, Environment and Performance: The Role of Strategic Choice', *Sociology*, 6, 1–22.

Child, J. and Czeglédy, A. P. (1996) 'Managerial Learning in the Transformation of Eastern Europe: Some Key Issues', *Organization Studies*, 17(2), 167–80.

Cole, R. E. (1973) 'Functional Alternatives and Economic Development: An Empirical Example of Permanent Employment in Japan', *American Sociology Review*, 38; 424–38.

Chou, T.-C. (1995) *Industrial Organisation in a Dichotomous Economy* (Aldershot: Avebury).

Chow, I. H. (1992) 'Chinese Managerial Work', *Journal of General Management*, 17(4), 53–67.

Clark, T. and Pugh, D. S. (1998) 'Convergence and Divergence in European HRM: An Exploratory Polycentric Study', Management Centre, King's College, University of London Working Paper.

Clegg, J. (1996) 'The Investment Development Path: Some Conclusions', in J. H. Dunning and R. Narula (eds), *Foreign Direct Investment and Governments* (London: Routledge), 42–77.

Copeland, A. (1995) 'Helping Foreign Nationals Adapt to the US', *Personnel Journal*, February, 83–7.

Crookell, H. H. (1986) 'Specialisation and International Competitiveness', in H. Etemad and L. S. Sulude (eds), *Managing the Multinational Subsidiary* (London: Croom Helm).

Crouch, C. and Streeck, W. (1997) 'Introduction: The Future of Capitalist Diversity', in C. Crouch and W. Streeck (eds), *Political Economy of Modern Capitalism* (London: Sage), 1–18.

Crozier, M. (1964) *The Bureaucratic Phenomenon* (London: Tavistock).

Cumings, B. (1987) 'The Origins and Development of the Northeast Asian Political Economy', in F. C. Deyo (ed.), *The Political Economy of the New Asian Industrialism* (Ithaca, N.Y.: Cornell University Press).

Cunningham, R. B. and Sarayrah, Y. K. (1993) *Wasta: The Hidden Force in Middle Eastern Society* (Westport, Conn.: Praeger).

Das, H. (1991) 'The Nature of Managerial Work in India: A Preliminary Investigation', *ASCI Journal of Management*, 12(1), 1–13.

Denison, D. R. (1990) *Corporate Culture and Organizational Effectiveness* (New York: Wiley).

Dore, R. (1997) 'The Distinctiveness of Japan', in C. Crouch and W. Streeck (eds), *Political Economy of Modern Capitalism* (London: Sage), 19–32.

Doz, Y. (1976) *National Policies and Multinational Management*, DBA dissertation, cited in J. Roure, J. A. Alvarez, C. Garcia-Pont and J. Nueno (1993), 'Managing International Dimensions of the Managerial Task', *European Management Journal*, 11, 485–92.

Dubin, R. (1970) 'Management in Britain – Impressions of a Visiting Professor', *Journal of Management Studies*, 7(2), 183–98.

Dunning, J. H. (1980) 'Toward an Eclectic Theory of International Production: Some Empirical Tests', *Journal of International Business Studies*, 11, Spring/Summer, 9–30.

Dunning, J. H. (1988) 'The Eclectic Paradigm of International Production; A Restatement and Some Possible Extensions', *Journal of International Business Studies*, 19, 1–31.

Economist Intelligence Unit (1992) *Building Brand Identity in Central Europe and the Former Soviet Union*, Report no. P802 (London: The Economist Group).

Enthoven, A. J. H. (1977) *Accounting in Third World Countries* (Amsterdam: North-Holland).

Fomburn, C., Tichy, N. M. and Devanna, M. A. (1984) *Strategic Human Resource Management* (Canada: Wiley).

Foreman-Peck, J. (1983) *A History of the World Economy* (Brighton: Wheatsheaf Books).

Form, W. (1979) 'Comparative Industrial Sociology and the Convergence Hypothesis', *Annual Review of Sociology*, 5, 1–25.

Forsgren, M. and Johanson, J. (1992) *Managing Networks in International Business* (Philadelphia: Gordon & Breach).

Francis, A. (1992) 'The Process of National Industrial Regeneration and Competitiveness', *Strategic Management Journal*, 13, 61–78.

Gee, S. (1993) 'Global Restructuring and Economic Development Strategies in Taiwan and South Korea', in C. Brundenius and B. Goransson (eds), *New Technologies and Global Restructuring* (London: Taylor Graham).

Ghoshal, S. (1986) *The Innovative Multinational: A Differentiated Network of Organizational Roles and Management Processes*', unpublished doctoral dissertation, Boston: Harvard Business School.

Ghoshal, S. and Bartlett, C. A. (1990) 'The Multinational Corporation as an Interorganizational Network', *Academy of Management Review*, 15(4), 603–25.

Ghoshal, S. and Bartlett, C. A. (1992) 'What is a Global Manager?', *Harvard Business Review*, 92, 124–32.

Gold, T. B. (1988) 'Entrepreneurs, Multinationals and the State', in E. A. Winckler and S. Greenhalgh (eds), *Contending Approaches to the Political Economy of Taiwan* (Armonk, N.Y.: M. E. Sharpe).

Gordon, C. (1990) 'The Business Culture in the United Kingdom', in C. Randlesome (ed.), *Business Cultures in Europe* (Oxford: Heinemann Professional).

Govindarajan, V. and Gupta, A. (1998a) 'Success is All in the Mindset', *Financial Times*, 27 October, survey page 2.

Govindarajan, V. and Gupta, A. (1998b) 'Setting a Course for the New Global Landscape', *Financial Times*, 30 January, survey page 3.

Hagen, S. (1988) *Languages in British Business* (Newcastle: Newcastle-upon-Tyne Polytechnic).

Haggard, S. (1988) 'The Politics of Industrialization in the Republic of Korea and Taiwan', in H. Hughes (ed.), *Achieving Industrialization in East Asia* (Cambridge: Cambridge University Press).

Håkanson, L. (1995) 'Learning through Acquisitions', *International Studies of Management and Organization*, 25(1), 121–57.

Hall, E. T. (1989) *The Dance of Life: The Other Dimension of Time* (New York: Doubleday).

Hall, R. (1993) 'A Framework linking Intangible Resources and Capabilities to Sustainable Competition Advantage', *Strategic Management Journal*, 14, 607–18.

Hall, E. T. and Hall, M. R. (1990) *Understanding Cultural Differences* (Yarmouth, Maine: Intercultural Press).

Hallén, L. and Weidersheim-Paul, F. (1979) 'Psychic Distance and Buyer–Seller Interaction', *Organisasjon, Marked og Samfund*, 16(3) 308–24, reprinted in English in Buckley, P. and Ghauri, P. (1999) *The Internationalisation of the Firm: A Reader*, 2nd edn (London: International Thompson).

Hamel, G. and Prahalad, C. (1990) 'The Core Competency of the Corporation', *Harvard Business Review*, 68(2), 79–91.

Hamilton, G. (1989) 'The Organizational Foundations of Western and Chinese Commerce', paper presented to the International Conference on Business Groups and Economic Development in East Asia, University of Hong Kong, 20–22 June.

Handy, C. (1988) 'Great Britain', in C. Handy, C. Gordon, I. Gow and C. Randlesome, *Making Managers* (London: Pitman).

Harvey, M. G. and Buckley, M. R. (1997) 'Managing Inpatriates: Building a Global Core Competency', *Journal of World Business*, 32(1), 35–52.

Hatton, W. (1995) *The State We're In* (London: Jonathan Cape).

Heenan, D. A. and Perlmutter, H. (1979) *Multinational Organization Development* (Reading, Mass.: Addison-Wesley).

Henderson, H. (1999) *The Changing Fortunes of Economic Liberalism* (London: Institute of Economic Affairs).

Hendry, C. and Pettigrew, A. (1990) 'Human Resource Management: An Agenda for the 1990s', *International Journal of Human Resource Management*, 1(1), 17–44.

Hickson, D. J., Hinnings, C. R., McMillan, C. J. M. and Schwitter, J. P. (1974) 'The Culture-Free Context of Organization Structure: A Tri-National Comparison', *Sociology*, 8, 59–80.

Hodgson, A. (1987) 'Deming's Never-ending Road to Quality', *Personnel Management*, July.

Hofstede, G. (1978) 'Culture and Organization: A Literature Review Study', *Journal of Enterprise Management*, 1, 127–35.

Hofstede, G. (1980) *Culture's Consequences* (California: Sage).

Hofstede, G. (1994) 'The Business of International Business is Culture', *International Business Review*, 3, 1–14.

Hofstede, G. (1998) 'Attitudes, Values and Organizational Culture; Disentangling the Concepts', *Organization Studies*, 19(3), 477–92.

Hofstede, G., Neuijen, B. and Ohavy, D. (1990) 'Measuring Organizational Cultures: A Qualitative and Quantitative Study across Twenty Cases', *Administrative Science Quarterly*, 35, 286–316.

Horovitz, J. and Kumar, N. (1998) 'Strategies for Retail Globalisation', *Financial Times*, 13 March, survey page 4.

Howells, J. and Michie, J. (1997) 'Technological Competitiveness in an International Arena', in J. Howells and J. Michie (eds), *Technology, Innovation and Competitiveness* (Cheltenham: Edward Elgar), 222–9.

Hsu, Y.-R. (1999) *'Recruitment and Selection and Human Resource Management in the Taiwanese Cultural Context'*, unpublished PhD thesis, University of Plymouth.

Hulbert, J. M. and Brandt, W. K. (1980) *Managing the Multinational Subsidiary* (New York: Holt, Rinehart & Winston).

Huntington, S. P. (1993) 'The Clash of Civilisations?' *Foreign Affairs*, 72(3), 22–49.

Huntington, S. P. (1996) *The Clash of Civilisations and the Remaking of World Order* (New York: Simon & Schuster).

Jamieson, I. (1980) *Capitalism and Culture: A Comparative Study of British and American Manufacturing Organisations* (Farnbourgh: Gower).

Jankowicz, A. D. (1994) 'The New Journey to Jerusalem: Mission and Meaning in the Managerial Crusade to Eastern Europe', *Organization Studies*, 15, 479–507.

Johanson, J. and Vahlne, J.-E. (1977) 'The Internationalisation Process of the Firm: A Model of Knowledge Development on Increasing Foreign Commitments', *Journal of International Business Studies*, 8(1), 23–32.

Johanson, J. and Wiedersheim-Paul, F. (1975) 'The Internationalization of the Firm: Four Swedish Cases', *Journal of Management Studies*, October, 305–22.

Johri, C. K. (1992) *Industrialism and Employment Systems in India* (Delhi: Oxford University Press).

Jones, L. and Sakong, I. (1980) *Government, Business and Entrepreneurship in Economic Development: The Korean Case* (Cambridge, Mass.: Harvard University Press).

Julius, D. (1990) *Global Companies and Public Policy* (London: Pinter).

Kanuango, R. N. and Mendonca, M. (1994) *Work Motivation: Models for Developing Countries* (New Delhi: Sage).

Kerr, C. J., Dunlop, J. T., Harbison, F. H. and Myers, C. A. (1952) *Industrialism and Industrial Man* (Cambridge, MA: Harvard University Press).

Kim, K.-D. (1988) 'The Distinctive Features of South Korea's Development', in P. L. Berger and H.-H. M. Hsiao (eds), *In Search of an East Asian Development Model* (New Brunswick, N.J.: Transaction).

Kleinke, C. L. (1984) 'Two Models for Conceptualizing the Attitude–Behaviour Relationship', *Human Relations*, 37, 333–50.

Kogut, B. and Singh, H. (1988) 'The Effect of National Culture on the Choice of Entry Mode', *Journal of International Business Studies*, Fall, 411–32.

Kuratko, D. F., Montagno, R. V. and Hornsby, J. S. (1990) 'Developing an Intrapreneurial Assessment Instrument for an Effective Corporate Entrepreneurial Environment, *Strategic Management Journal*, 11, 49–58.

Laczniak, G. R. and Murphy, P. R. (1993) *Ethical Marketing Decisions: The Higher Road* (Boston: Allyn & Bacon).

Lall, S. (1996) 'The Investment Development Path: Some Conclusions', in J. H. Dunning and R. Narula (eds), *Foreign Direct Investment and Governments* (London: Routledge), 423–41.

Landes, D. (1998) *The Wealth and Poverty of Nations* (London: W. W. Norton).

Lane, C. (1995) *Industry and Society in Europe: Stability and Change in Britain, Germany and France* (Aldershot: Edward Elgar).

Latifi, F. (1997) 'Management Learning in National Context', unpublished PhD thesis, Henley Management College.

Laurent, A. (1983) 'The Cultural Diversity of Western Management Conceptions', *International Studies of Management and Organizations*, 8, 75–96.

Laurent, A. (1986) 'The Cross-Cultural Puzzle of International Human Resource Management', *Human Resource Management*, 25, 91–102.

Lawrence, P. and Lorsch, J. (1967) *Organizations and Environment* (Cambridge, Mass.: Harvard University Press).

Legge, K. (1989) 'Human Resource Management: A Critical Analysis', in J. Storey (ed.), *New Perspectives on Human Resource Management* (London: Routledge), 19–40.

Legge, K. (1995) *Human Resource Management: Rhetorics and Realities* (Basingstoke: Macmillan).

Lehmann, J. (1998) 'Who Writes Today's Economic Scripts?', *Financial Times*, 27 March, survey page 2.

Lincoln, J., Hanada, M. and Olson, J. (1981) 'Cultural Orientations and Individual Reactions to Organizations: A Study of Employees of Japanese-Owned Firms', *Administrative Science Quarterly*, 26(1), 93–115.

Locke, B. (1985) 'The Relationship Between Educational and Managerial Cultures in Britain and West Germany', in P. Joynt and M. Warner (eds) *Managing in Different Cultures* (Oslo: Universitetsforlaget).

Locke, R. R. (1996) *The Collapse of the American Management Mystique* (Oxford: Oxford University Press).

Macduffie, J. P. (1995) 'Human Resource Bundles and Manufacturing Performance: Organizational Logic and Flexible Production Systems in the World Auto Industry', *Industrial Labor Relations Review*, 48, 197–221.

Macquin, A. and Rouzies, D. (1998) 'Selling Across the Culture Gap', *Financial Times*, 13 March, survey page 10.

Maddison, A. (1971) *Class Structure and Economic Growth, India and Pakistan since the Moghuls* (London: Allen & Unwin).

Mangham, I. L. (1978) *Interactions and Interventions in Organizations* (Chichester: Wiley).

Marlow, S. and Patten, D. (1993) 'Managing the Employment Relationship in the Smaller Firm: Possibilities for Human resource Management', *International Small Business Journal*, 11, 57–64.

Marr, A. (1995) *Ruling Britannia: The Failure and Future of British Democracy* (London: Michael Joseph).

Martin, J., Feldman, M. S., Hatch, M. J. and Sitkin, S. B. (1983) 'The Uniqueness Paradox in Organisational Stories', *Administrative Science Quarterly*, 28, 438–53.

Masakazu, Y. (1994) *Individualism and Japanese: An Alternative Approach to Cultural Comparison* (Tokyo: Japan Echo Inc.), translated by Barbara Sugihara.

Maslow, A. H. (1954) *Motivation and Personality* (New York: Harper & Row).

McFarlane, A. (1978) *The Origins of English Individualism* (Oxford: Basil Blackwell).

McKiernan, P. (1992) *Strategies of Growth: Maturity, Recovery and Internationalization* (London: Routledge).

McKinsey (consultancy firm) (1998) *Driving Productivity and Growth in the UK Economy*, report discussed on the BBC Radio 4 news programmes, 30 October 1998 and cited in *The Economist*, 31 October, 1998.

McClelland, D. C. (1961) *The Achieving Society* (Princeton, NJ: Nostrand).

Melin, L. (1997) 'Internationalisation as a Strategy Process', in H. Vernon-Wortzel and L. H. Wortzel (eds), *Strategic Management* (New York: Wiley & Sons).

Meyer, J. W. and Rowan, B. (1977) 'Institutionalized Organizations: Formal Structure as Myth and Ceremony', *American Journal of Sociology*, 83, 340–63.

Michie, J. and Prendergast, R. (1997) 'Innovation and Competitive Advantage', in J. Howells and J. Michie (eds), *Technology, Innovation and Competitiveness* (Cheltenham: Edward Elgar), 203–21.

Mirza, H. (1998) 'Transnational Corporations as Agents for Transmission of Business Culture to Host Countries', in P. Cook, C. Kirkpatrick and F. Nixon (eds), *Privatization, Enterprise Development and Economic Reform* (Cheltenham: Edward Elgar), 33–62.

Moore, K. (1994) 'Capturing International Responsibilities in the Canadian Pharmaceutical Industry', *Industry Canada Working Paper* (Ottawa: Industry Canada).

Morgan, G. (1986) *Images of Organization* (California: Sage).

Mortazavi, S. and Karimi, E. (1990) 'Cultural Dimensions of Paternalistic Behaviour: A Cross-cultural Research in Five Countries', in S. Iwawaki, Y. Kashima and L. Kwok (eds), *Innovation in Cross-cultural Psychology* (Amsterdam, Berwyn, PA: Swets & Zeitlinger), 147–51.

Mortazavi, S. and Saheli, A. (1992) 'Organisational Culture, Paternalistic Leadership and Job Satisfaction in Iran', paper presented at the 22nd International Congress of Applied Psychology, Erlbaum, UK.

Muna, F. A. (1980) *The Arab Executive* (London: Macmillan).

Münchau, W. (1998) 'Costs: A Nation Totting up the Bill', *Financial Times* website, 5 January.

Nahapiet, J. (1998) 'Strategies for the Global Service', *Financial Times*, 6 February, survey page 10.

Nakane, C. (1973) *Japanese Society* (London: Penguin).

Negandhi, A. R. (1979) 'Convergence in Organizational Practices: An Empirical Study of Industrial Enterprise in Developing Countries', in C. J. Lammers and D. J. Hickson (ed.), *Organizations Alike and Unlike* (London: Routledge & Kegan Paul), pp. 323–45.

Negandhi, A. R. (1985) 'Management in the Third World', in Pat Joynt and Malcolm Warner (ed.), *Managing in Different Cultures* (Oslo: Universitetsforlaget), pp. 69–97.

Nicholaidis, C. S. (1992) *'Cultural Determinants of Corporate Excellence: The Impact of National Cultures on Organisational Performance'*, unpublished PhD thesis, University of Reading.

Nordström, K. A. and Vahlne, J.-E. (1992) 'Is the Globe Shrinking? Psychic Distance and the Establishment of Swedish Sales Subsidiaries during the Last 100 Years', paper presented at the International Trade and Finance Association's Annual Conference, April 22–25, Laredo, Texas.

O'Grady, S. and Lane, H. W. (1996) 'The Psychic Distance Paradox', *Journal of International Business Studies*, 27(2), 309–33.

Oliver, N. and Davies, A. (1990), 'Adopting Japanese-style Manufacturing Methods: A Tale of Two (UK) Factories', *Journal of Management Studies*, 27, 555–70.

Oliver, N. and Wilkinson, B. (1992), *Japanization of British Industry* (Oxford: Blackwell).

O'Mahony, M. (1998) 'Britain's Relative Productivity Performance, 1950–96: A Sectoral Analysis' (London: National Institute of Economic and Social Research and Economic and Social Research council), September.

Orru, M. (1991) 'Business Organizations in a Comparative Perspective: Small Firms in Taiwan and Italy', *Studies in Comparative International Development*, 26.

Osterman, P. (1994) 'How Common is Workplace Transformation and Who Adopts It?', *Industrial and Labor Relations Review*, 42, 173–88.

Patten, C. (1998) 'Of Tigers, Bulls and Bears', *Time*, 2 February 1998, 56–7.

Pechter, K. (1993) 'The Foreigners are Coming', *International Business*, September, 55–60.

Perlmutter, H. (1969) 'The Tortuous Evolution of the Multinational Corporation', *Columbia Journal of World Business*, 4, 9–18.

Peters, T. J. and Waterman, R. H. (1982) *In Search of Excellence* (New York: Harper & Row).

Petty, R. E. (1981) 'The Role of Cognitive Responses in Attitude Change Processes', in R. E. Petty, T. M. Ostrom and T. C. Brock (eds), *Cognitive Responses in Persuasion* (Hillsdale, N.J.: Erlbaum).

Poole, M. (1990) 'Human Resource Management in an International Perspective', *International Journal of Human Reource Management*, 1(1), 1–15.

Porter, M. E. (1990) *The Competitive Advantage of Nations* (Basingstoke: Macmillan).

Poynter, T. A. and Rugman, A. R. (1982) 'World Product Mandates: How Will Multinationals Respond?', *Business Quarterly*, 46 (Fall), 54–61.

Prahalad, C. K. (1976) 'Strategic Choices in Diversified MNCs', *Harvard Business Review*, July–August, 67–78.

Pralahad, C. K. and Doz, Y. L. (1987) *The Multinational Mission: Balancing Global Demands and Global Vision* (New York: Free Press).

Pucik, V. (1998) 'Creating Leaders that are World-Class, *Financial Times*, February, survey page 4.

Reader, J. (1997) *Africa: A Biography of a Continent* (London: Hamish Hamilton).

Reid, D. M. (1989) 'Operationalizing Strategic Planning', *Strategic Management Journal*, 10(6), 553–67.

Reid, S. D. (1986) 'Export Channel Choice and Export Performance: A Contingency Approach', in C. Tan, W. Lazer and V. Kirpalani (eds), *Emerging International Strategic Frontiers* (Singapore: American Marketing Association), 260–4.

Ritzer, G. (1996) *The McDonaldization of Society: An Investigation into the Changing Character of Contemporary Social Life*, revd edn (London: Pine Forge).

Robock, S. H. and Simmonds, K. (1983) *International Business and Multinational Enterprise* (Homewood Cliffs, Illinois: Prentice-Hall).

Roderick, G. and Stephens, M. D. (1978) *Education and Industry in the Nineteenth Century: The English Disease* (London: Longman).

Roderick, G. and Stephens, M. D. (1981) *Where Did We Go Wrong?: Industry, Education and Economy of Victorian Britain* (London: The Falmer Press).

Roderick, G. and Stephens, M. D. (1982) *The British Malaise; Industrial Performance, Education and Training in Britain Today* (London: The Falmer Press).

Roney, J. (1997) 'Cultural Implications of Implementing TQM in Poland', *Journal of World Business*, 32(2), 152–68.

Root, F. R. (1987) *Entry Strategies for International Markets* (Lexington, Mass.: Lexington Books).

Rosenzweig, P. (1994) 'Why is Managing in the United States so Difficult for European Firms?', *European Management Journal*, 12, 31–8.

Roth, K. and Morrison, A. J. (1992) 'Implementing Global Strategy: Characteristics of Global Subsidiary Mandates, *Journal of International Business Studies*, 23(4), 715–36.

Rowen, H. S. (1998) 'The Political and Social Foundations of the Rise of East Asia: An Overview', in S. H. Rowen (ed.), *Behind East Asian Growth* (London: Routledge), 1–38.

Rugman, A. M. (1980) 'A New Theory of Multinational Enterprise: Internationalization verus Internalization', *Columbia Journal of World Business*, 15, 23–9.

Rugman, A. M. (1998) 'Multinationals as Regional Flagships', *Financial Times*, 30 January, survey page 6.

Rugman, A. M. and Gestrin, M. (1993) 'The Strategic Response to Multinational Enterprises to NAFTA', *Columbia Journal of World Business*, 24(1), 18–29.

Sathe, V. (1983) 'Implications of Corporate Culture: A Managers Guide to action', *Organisational Dynamics* (Autumn), 5–23.

Sayigh, Y. A. (1982) *The Arab Economy: Past performance and Future Prospects* (New York: Oxford University Press).

Schein, E. H. (1985) *Organizational Culture and Leadership: A Dynamic View* (San Francisco: Jossey-Bass).

Schuler, R. S., Dowling, P. J. and De Cieri, H. (1993) 'An Integrative Framework of Strategic International Human Resource Management', *Journal of Management*, 19, 419–59.

Segalla, M. (1998) 'National Cultures, International Business', *Financial Times*, 7 March, survey page 8.

Seizaburo, S. (1997) 'Clash of Civilisations or Cross-Fertilization of Civilisations?', *Japan Echo*, October, 44–9, translated from 'Bunmei no shdtotsu ka, sogo gakushu ka', in *Asuteion*, Summer 1997, 28–39; slightly abridged.

Shadur, M. A., Rodwell, J. J., Bamber, G. J. and Simmons, D. E. (1995) 'The Adoption of International Best Practices in a Western Culture: East meets West', *International Journal of Human Resource Management*, 6, 735–57.

Sharma, S. D. (1992) 'The Policies and Politics of Rural development and the Limits to Reform and Redistribution: The Case of Post-Independence India', unpublished PhD thesis, University of Toronto.

Shirai, T. (1983) *Contemporary Industrial Relations in Japan* (Madison: University of Wisconsin Press).

Silverman, D. (1970) *The Theory of Organizations* (London: Heinemann).

Singer, H. and Ansari, J. (1982) *Rich and Poor Countries*, 3rd edn (Winchester, Mass.: George Allen & Unwin).

Smith, P. B., Dugan, S. and Trompenaars, F. (1996) 'National Culture and the Values of Organisational Employees: A Dimensional Analaysis across 43 Nations', *Journal of Cross-cultural Psychology*, 27, 231–64.

Solberg, C. A. (1998) 'Buyer Behaviour in Arab Organisations', paper presented to the Conference on Globalization, the International Firm and Emerging Economies, 27 May–1 June, Izmir, Turkey.

Stajovic, A. D. and Luthans, F. (1997) 'Business Ethics across Cultures: A Social Cognitive Model', *Journal of World Business*, 32(1), 17–34.

Storey, J. (1987) 'Developments in the Management of Human Resources: An Interim Report', Warwick Papers in Industrial Relations, no. 17, IRRU, School of Industrial and Business Studies, University of Warwick, November.

Storey, J. (1992) *Developments in Management of Human Resources* (Oxford: Blackwell).

Taka, I. and Foglia, W. D. (1994) 'Ethical Aspects of Japanese Leadership Style', *Business Ethics*, 13, 135–48.

Tayeb, M. H. (1979) 'Cultural Determinants of Organizational Response to Environmental Demands: An Empirical Study in Iran', unpublished M. Litt. thesis, University of Oxford.

Tayeb, M. H. (1988) *Organizations and National Culture: A Comparative Analysis* (London: Sage).

Tayeb, M. H. (1990) 'Japanese Management Style', in R. Daily, *Organisational Behaviour* (London: Pitman), 257–82.

Tayeb, M. H. (1993) 'English Culture and Business Organisations', in D. J. Hickson (ed.), *Management in Western Europe* (Berlin: Walter de Gruyter), 47–64.

Tayeb, M. H. (1994) 'Japanese Managers and British Culture: A Comparative Case Study', *International Journal of Human Resource Management*, 5(1), 145–66.

Tayeb, M. H. (1995) 'The Competitive Advantage of Nations: The Role of HRM and its Socio-cultural Context', *International Journal of Human Resource Management*, 6, 588–605.

Tayeb, M. H. (1996a) *The Management of a Multicultural Workforce* (Chichester: Wiley & Sons).

Tayeb, M. H. (1996b) 'India: A Non-Tiger of Asia', *International Business Review*, 5(5), 425–45.

Tayeb, M. H. (1997) 'Islamic Revival in Asia and Human Resource Management', *Employee Relations*, 9(4), 352–64.

Tayeb, M. H. (1998) 'Transfer of HRM Policies and Practices across Cultures: An American Company in Scotland', *International Journal of Human Resource Management*, 9(2), 332–58.

Tayeb, M. H. (1999a) 'Management in Iran', in M. Warner (ed.), *International Encyclopaedia of Business and Management – Regional Set* (London: International Thomson Business Press).

Tayeb, M. H. (1999b) 'Foreign Remedies for Local Difficulties: The Case of Three Scottish Manufacturing Firms', to appear in the *International Journal of Human Resource Management*, 10(5), 842–57.

Tayeb, M. H. and Dott, E. (2000) 'Two Nations Divided by a Common Language: Three American Companies in Scotland', to appear in *International Studies of Management and Organization*.

Terry, P. (1979) 'An Investigation of Some Cultural Determinants of English Organization Behaviour', unpublished PhD thesis, University of Bath.

Thomas, T. (1994) 'Change in Climate for Foreign Investment in India', *Columbia Journal of World Business*, 29(1), 32–40.

Thorelli, H. B. (1981) 'Consumer Policy for the Third World', *Journal of Consumer Policy*, 5(3), 197–211.

Thorelli, H. B. and Sentell, G. D. (1982) *Consumer Emancipation and Economic Development: The Case of Thailand* (Greenwich, Conn.: Jai Press).

Thornhill, A. (1993) 'Management Training Across Cultures: The Challenge for Trainers', *Journal of European Industrial Training*, 17(10), 43–51.

Toyne, B. (1989) 'International Exchange: A Foundation for Theory Building in International Business', *Journal of International Business Studies*, 20, 1–17.

Trice, H. M. and Beyer, J. M. (1984) 'Studying Organisational Cultures through Rites and Ceremonials', *Academy of Management Review*, 9, 653–9.

Trinque, B. M. (1993) 'Challenge–Response Mechanism and Unmodal Strategy: Inertia and Options in India's Economic Development', unpublished PhD thesis, University of Texas at Austin.

Trought, B. (1989) 'A Comparison of the Work Activity of Quality Assurance and Production Managers', *International Journal of Quality and Reliability Management*, 6(2), 25–30.

Tung, R. L. (1984) *Key to Japan's Economic Strength: Human Power* (Lexington, Mass.: D. C. Heath).

Tung, R. L. (1988) *The New Expatriates* (Cambridge, Mass.: Ballinger).

Tunstall, W. B. (1983) 'Cultural Transition at AT&T', *Sloan Management Review*, 25, 15–26.

Turnbull, P. (1986) 'The "Japanisation" of Production and Industrial Relations at Lucas Electrical', *Industrial Relations Journal*, 17, 193–206.

Tyson, S. and Fell, A. (1986) *Evaluating the Personnel Function* (London: Hutchinson).

Vaughan, E. (1994) 'The Trial between Sense and Sentiment: A Reflection on the Language of HRM', *Journal of General Management*, 19, 20–32.

Vernon, R. (1966) 'International Investment and International Trade in the Product Cycle', *Quarterly Journal of Economics*, 80 (May), 190–207.

Vikhanski, O. and Puffer, S. (1993) 'Management Education and Employee Training at Moscow McDonald's', *European Management Journal*, 11, 102–7.

Vineall, T. (1988) 'Creating a Multinational Management Team', *Personnel Management*, October, 44–7.

Wade, R. (1990) *Governing the Market* (Princeton: Princeton University Press).

Walton, R. E. (1985) 'Towards a Strategy of Eliciting Employee Commitment Based on Policies of Mutuality', in R. E. Walton and P. R. Lawrence (eds), *Human Resource Management: Trends and Challenges* (Boston, Mass.: Harvard Business School Press), 35–65.

Watson, J. (1998) *Golden Arches East: McDonald's in East Asia* (Cambridge: Cambridge University Press).

Weber, M. (1930) *The Protestant Ethic and the Spirit of Capitalism* (London: George Allen & Unwin).

West, P. (1989) 'Cross-Cultural Literacy and the Pacific Rim', *Business Horizon*, March–April, 3–17.

Welch, D. (1994) 'HRM Implications of Globalization', *Journal of General Management*, 19, 52–68.

Wells, L. T. (1968) 'A Product Life-cycle for International Trade', *Journal of Marketing*, 32, 1–6.

Wheeler, C., Jones, M. and Young, S. (1996) 'Market Entry Modes and Channels of Distribution in the Machine Tool Industry in the UK', *European Journal of Marketing*, 34(4), 40–57.

Whitley, R. (1992) *Business Systems in East Asia* (London: Sage).

Whittington, R. (1990) 'Social Structures and Resistance to Strategic Change: British Manufacturers in the 1980s', *British Journal of Management*, 1(4), 201–14.

Wiener, M. J. (1981) *English Culture and the Decline of the Industrial Spirit: 1850–1980* (London: Cambridge University Press).

Wilson, D. C. and Rosenfeld, R. H. (1990) *Managing Organizations* (London: McGraw-Hill).

World Bank (1993) *East Asian Miracle* (Washington: The World Bank).

World Bank (1997) *Development Report 1997* (Washington: The World Bank).

Yoshimori, M. (1995) 'Whose Company Is It? The Concept of Corporation in Japan and the West', *Long Range Planning*, 28(4), 33–4.

Young, H. (1998) *This Blessed Plot* (London: Macmillan).

Young, S. (1987) 'Business Strategy and the Internationalization of Business: Recent Approaches', *Managerial and Decision Economics*, 8, 31–40.

Zeile, W. (1989) 'Industrial Policy and Organizational Efficiency: The Korean Chaebol Examined', Program in East Asia Business and Development Research Working Paper No. 30, Institute of Governmental Affairs, University of California, Davis.

Index